T0305376

THE MYTH OF MILLIONAIRE TAX FLIGHT

STUDIES IN SOCIAL INEQUALITY

This book series is devoted to examining poverty and inequality in its many forms, including the takeoff in economic inequality, increasing spatial segregation, and ongoing changes in gender, racial, and ethnic inequality.

THE MYTH OF MILLIONAIRE TAX FLIGHT

How Place Still Matters for the Rich

CRISTOBAL YOUNG

STANFORD UNIVERSITY PRESS
STANFORD, CALIFORNIA

Stanford University Press
Stanford, California

Printed in the United States of America on acid-free, archival-quality paper

Library of Congress Cataloging-in-Publication Data

Names: Young, Cristobal, author.
Title: The myth of millionaire tax flight : how place still matters for the rich / Cristobal Young.
Description: Stanford, California : Stanford University Press, 2018. | Series: Studies in social inequality | Includes bibliographical references and index.
Identifiers: LCCN 2017015547 (print) | LCCN 2017020482 (ebook) | ISBN 9781503603813 (e-book) | ISBN 9781503601147 (cloth : alk. paper) | ISBN 9781503603806 (pbk. : alk. paper)
Subjects: LCSH: Rich people--Taxation--United States. | Migration, Internal--United States. | Place attachment--United States. | Rich people--Taxation. | Tax havens. | Emigration and immigration. | Place attachment.
Classification: LCC HJ4653.R6 (ebook) | LCC HJ4653.R6 Y68 2017 (print) | DDC 336.20086/210973--dc23
LC record available at https://lccn.loc.gov/2017015547

Cover design: Preston Thomas, Cadence Design
Typeset by Bruce Lundquist in 10/15 Minion Pro

Table of Contents

List of Figures   vii

Acknowledgments   ix

1. Millionaire Taxes in a World with Few Borders   1

2. Do the Rich Flee High Taxes?   15

3. Global Billionaires and International Tax Havens   43

4. Place as a Form of Capital   67

5. Millionaires and the Future of Taxation   97

Notes   113

References   121

Index   133

List of Figures

Figure 2.1. Millionaire Concentration and Top State Tax Rates,
1999 to 2011   21

Figure 2.2. Migration Rates by Income Level, 1999 to 2011   22

Figure 2.3. Border Counties of Washington and Oregon   29

Figure 2.4. Border Counties and Tax Differences in the United States   30

Figure 2.5. Forbes Billionaire Population Per Capita,
by Top State Income Tax Rate, 2010   33

Figure 2.6. Millionaire Migration Rates, by Socioeconomic Group 36

Figure 2.7. Migration Rates by Age, for Different Levels of Education   39

Figure 3.1. Demographics of Global Migration, 2010   46

Figure 3.2. Retention of Billionaires by Country and Tax Rate, 2010   47

Figure 3.3. Retention of Billionaires by Country and
Per Capita GDP, 2010   50

Figure 3.4. Use of Offshore Accounts   63

Figure 4.1. Foreign Population in Western Europe (EU15),
1995 to 2014   90

Acknowledgments

Writing a book is to live a life absorbed in writing. I have been fortunate to have exceptional companions and collaborators in this task. One of the central themes of the book is that no accomplishment is an individual act—everything we do is a joint product, and all our work is the result of team production. And every so often, we have the chance to reflect on, honor, and thank those who helped us achieve our best work. It is a pleasure to do so here.

I have been studying and writing about millionaire migration for many years. But I only began writing this book while teaching a "third-year paper seminar" at Stanford in the fall of 2015. This course made me responsible for twelve graduate students, and I pushed them hard to do their best in writing weekly memos and in developing the broader vision of their projects. I soon came to want the same demands and discipline placed on me and reached out for help. My wife Patricia became the patient but demanding reader of my own weekly memos. I also reached out to my colleagues Alice Goffman and Sarah Quinn, and together we formed a book-writing club that kept the deadlines real and the feedback insightful. So began a year of intensive writing.

The initial project of millionaire migration began in collaboration with Charles Varner back in 2008. Charles was my colleague in sociology at Princeton and is now executive director of the Stanford Center on Poverty and Inequality. We have done far more together than I ever could have accomplished alone. Charles is a true scientist and a relentless voice for diligence. We shared a vision of science and a conviction of purpose in our work. Our progress was slow sometimes—because we had a lot to learn, felt a deep responsibility to get it right, and endlessly triple-checked our results. It is hard to imagine having a better research partner in this project. Our years of working together deeply inform this book. I thank him for every bit of energy he has given to our work.

I am also indebted to Ithai Lurie and Rich Prisinzano at the U.S. Department of the Treasury, who curated my access to the IRS tax return data. The confidential tax returns of American citizens provide the core empirical foundation for this book, especially the 45 million tax returns of the richest U.S. citizens over more than a decade. Legally, I have no access to the raw tax return data, and I cannot even enter the building where these data are housed. These data are highly sensitive and deserve careful protections. Over several years, Ithai and Rich made these data available remotely in analytical results. I sent them statistical code, and they sent back statistical findings. This may sound like an easy process, but it required tremendous patience from everyone. A missing semicolon can render well-designed code useless and hard to debug. Statistical code sent by e-mail is hard to write, and hard to implement, with error sources that are hard to guess at. There were times when all of us wondered whether this collaboration was worth the painstaking effort it required. But it was, and I gratefully thank Ithai and Rich for the years they put into this project. I would gladly do it all over again for what has been learned and hope that the tax data will continue to be available to scholars with important questions to ask.

Maddy Young was my graduate research assistant while writing this book, and it was a privilege to have her energy and commitment to the project. She helped with the research and data collection but was soon promoted to book editor. Maddy has a piercing eye for clarity and detail, combined with a kindness of form, that made me eager to read her feedback and questions. I also had excellent research assistance from Katharina Roesler, Andrew Granato, and Erin Cumberworth. Their assistance has turned what could have been a long, hard slog into an exciting process of discovery. I thank each of them for their contributions.

Many people over the years have shared their thoughts, feedback, and input on this project, including Woody Powell, Bruce Carruthers, Mark Granovetter, Mitchell Stevens, Monica Prasad, Emmanuel Saez, Mike Hout, David Grusky, Jeff Manza, Shamus Khan, Paul Starr, David Pedulla, Marty

Gilens, Eric Schwartz, Emily Erikson, Pablo Mitnik, Isaac Martin, Dan Lichter, Philip Morgan, Deirdre Bloome, Jerald Herting, Emilio Zagheni, Christof Brandtner, Jennifer Hill, Aaron Horvath, Sarah Thébaud, Mark Mizruchi, Filiz Garip, and Gabriel Rossman. At Stanford, I have enjoyed a community of scholars and supporters including Shelley Correll, Michelle Jackson, Tomás Jiménez, Michael Rosenfeld, Paolo Parigi, Aliya Saperstein, Amir Goldberg, and Corey Fields. I am grateful to all of you for your friendship and for the many small and kind ways you helped make both work and life better.

From Princeton University, where I first began this work, I want to thank the people who helped give me the strongest possible start, including Paul DiMaggio, Douglas Massey, Martin Ruef, Viviana Zelizer, Bruce Western, Scott Lynch, and Robert Wuthnow. I'm thankful for their support and encouragement and miss the many great conversations we had.

At Stanford University Press, I thank Paula England and Kate Wahl for their support and confidence in the book project. I also thank anonymous reviewers for their excellent feedback on both the initial proposal and the submitted manuscript.

Finally, my wife Patricia has been my companion in life, love, and scholarship for more than fifteen years. Few ideas are distilled in my mind without Patricia's guidance and filter. Few parts of my life are meaningful without her presence. She is the center of my life, and my anchor. I dedicate this book to her.

THE MYTH OF MILLIONAIRE TAX FLIGHT

1

Millionaire Taxes in a World with Few Borders

We live in a time of both globalization and growing inequality. This dual trend presents a troubling challenge. Places and nations can alleviate inequality, at least in part, by taxing the well-off and investing in education, infrastructure, and public services that make life better for most people. But globalization renders the rich more mobile and less connected to places that might tax them. The potential flight of the rich leaves places, states, and countries wondering about the future.

Many places and nations are concerned about the migration of top taxpayers. Taxes paid by the rich provide revenue for vital public services and help to address the growing inequality in market incomes. However, millionaire migration—the flight of the largest taxpayers—can drain state revenues and set off a race to the bottom as states try to woo the richest with ever-lower tax rates.

The discourse of globalization depicts a world where borders are frequently crossed. Rich, cosmopolitan elites and their capital flow easily across borders; people are less tied to place, less tied to the land, to their nation, and to their local communities. If this characterization is true, it is incredibly important. If a jet-setting millionaire class can easily dodge taxes by moving away, these people can effectively dictate tax policy to states and nations by threatening to leave.

In recent years, eight U.S. states have passed "millionaire taxes"—new income tax brackets with higher rates—on their highest income earners. Yet, some other U.S. states, like Texas and Florida, still have no state income tax at all. Can some states tax the rich while other states do not? Can higher tax states retain their wealthy residents and the tax revenue they bring in?

Many answer this question with a ferocious no. As Oregon residents went to the polls to vote on a proposed millionaire tax in 2010, Oregon's richest resident—Nike founder and chairman Phil Knight—warned that the tax would set off a "death spiral" in which "thousands of our most successful residents will leave the state."[1] In Maryland, Larry Hogan, a leading critic of the state's short-lived millionaire tax, insisted in 2012 that "people are simply going to leave, leading to a downward spiral of raising revenues on fewer citizens."[2] Hogan was subsequently elected as the Republican governor of Maryland. In New Jersey, Governor Chris Christie simply declared, "Ladies and gentlemen, if you tax them, they will leave."[3]

These views are based on the strength of people's convictions rather than actual evidence. Until very recently, there has been remarkably little data and analysis on the migration patterns of top income earners. Debates have been driven by anecdotes and instincts. This book is about filling in the vacuum of evidence—drawing on big data to provide compelling answers to a systematic set of questions about the mobility of the rich.

Top income earners—defined here as those making at least $1 million a year—are free to live anywhere in the United States. The very richest of them can likely live anywhere in the world. Indeed, for the rich today, the global map looks increasingly like the United States—a collection of places with no real borders between them, among which an economic elite can freely move and choose where to live.

With the diminishing cost of travel, increasing ease of obtaining international visas, and the rise of online communication, the viability of tax migration seems greater today than ever before. Some see the very richest as making up a "transnational capitalist class"[4] that enjoys unrestricted freedom to move across the world through a network of global cities. Will this compel states and countries to compete over lowering tax rates on the rich? Will low-tax states and nations poach the highest income earners from higher tax places? This issue is closely related to questions of how globalization, more generally, is disciplining nations and creating pressure for an international race to the bottom in taxation and social policy.

Neoclassical economists have long seen taxes as a factor that influences where people choose to live.[5] Economists, of course, also recognized that taxes pay for public goods—better roads, bridges, parks, and schools—that influence where people want to live. As long as revenues are used to fund public services that matter to residents, there is no reason to think taxes would lead to out-migration. However, in more recent years, some have argued that under highly progressive taxes, the rich contribute much more than they receive in public services. Harvard economist Martin Feldstein has made some of the strongest claims about tax migration among top earners. In a world of free mobility, Feldstein argues, taxes on the rich do not raise revenue or reduce inequality but simply lead to millionaire migration. If states raise taxes on the rich, the top income earners will leave, causing not just a loss of tax revenue but also a shortage of high-skill workers. The market will, in turn, bid up the wages of the remaining high-skill workers, and inequality in the state will return to its equilibrium level. Taxes on the rich, Feldstein argues, fail because of freedom of movement.[6] This view has become increasingly prominent in public debates over taxes, especially at the state level.

There are, however, broader sociological reasons to doubt the ready mobility of millionaires. Moving is a young person's game, but earning income in the top bracket is not. Migration overwhelmingly occurs when people are establishing their careers. People almost never move when they are at the advanced career stage—a time when they are most likely to face a millionaire tax. At the peaks of their careers, people have family responsibilities—spouses and children who may be opposed to moving. They also have a lot of business and social contacts that make them prominent, well-connected insiders where they live. Top income earners, in other words, have often accumulated significant human, social, and cultural capital where they live.

Economic sociologists have long emphasized that economic action, such as income earning, is "embedded in concrete, ongoing systems of social relations."[7] Income is partly based on personal connections to colleagues and clients, experience within a company, local reputation and goodwill, knowledge of one's competitors, and access to social networks that bring rich information. Moving after achieving high success or at a late career stage can mean giving up a home-field advantage that may not make much business or economic sense.

.　.　.

In the age of globalization, what is the connection between the rich and the places where they live? Is place a temporary convenience for the rich and powerful—readily switched out when the tides change? Or is place a deep foundation for their success? Are top income earners "mobile millionaires" searching for low-tax places to live, or are they "embedded elites" reluctant to move away from the places where they have become highly successful?

These questions are important because they can yield insight into the future of inequality in the United States. One of the biggest socioeconomic questions of our time is whether the United States can build a new era of shared prosperity. Can we make the engine of economic growth something that benefits everyone?

In recent decades, market economies have created a great deal of inequality. This is a story of middle-class wage stagnation, combined with dramatic gains in income at the top. The top 1 percent today capture more than 20 percent of all income created in the U.S. economy. This share has been growing rapidly. Since the early 1990s, roughly half of all income *growth* in the United States has accrued to the top 1 percent, with the other half going to the rest of the population—the 99 percent.[8] Corporate CEO salaries illustrate the extremes of the growing divergence in economic fortunes. Since 1978, real CEO salaries have increased roughly tenfold— from $1.5 million to $16 million per year—while average worker incomes have risen little more than 10 percent.[9] This is the rise of a winner-take-all economy, where the benefits of economic growth largely accrue to those at the top.

Rising inequality is not a generic feature of capitalism. In the years following World War II and into the late 1970s, tremendous economic growth was coupled with a *declining* share of income held by the top 1 percent. This was truly an era in which "a rising tide lifts all boats"—and middle-class boats were rising fastest. But the world—and the nature of economic life— has changed a great deal in the decades that followed. Those changes include the end of the Cold War, the computer revolution, globalization, trade deals, offshoring of jobs, the decline of private sector unions, the growth of Wall Street and financialization of the economy, eroding minimum wages, and the reduction of taxes on top incomes. The end result is that Americans are no longer living in an era of broadly shared prosperity.

It is easy to be pessimistic about our economic future. Thomas Piketty, in his book *Capital in the Twenty-First Century*, argues that the post-war era of economic growth and shared prosperity was an anomaly and that the future will entail a steadily rising concentration of wealth and power in society.[10] The rate of return on capital in the foreseeable future, Piketty argues, will be higher than the overall rate of economic growth. This means the rich— or, at least the owners of capital and their investment managers and advisors—will be getting richer at a faster rate than the rest of society and will be claiming a growing share of the overall dividends of a productive society.

Piketty calls for a global tax on wealth—although he himself presents it as a hypothetical ideal. We could think of the proposal as calling for a "World Tax Organization," operating alongside the World Trade Organization.[11] But there is no obvious pathway to such an international consensus. One problem is that the countries of the world—and even states within the United States—do not agree on what the top tax rate should be, and many places want different tax policies. In a time of globalization—and in a world with digital finance, shell companies, and easy mobility—tax flight and the migration of the elite are prominent concerns for policymakers. If some places have very low taxes, can other places sustain different policies that ask more of the top income earners?

Varieties of Taxation

Over the last several decades, U.S. national tax policy has shifted away from the taxation of the rich, sharply reducing tax rates on top incomes, capital gains, and multimillion-dollar inheritances. The U.S. anti-tax political movement has largely been a campaign to "untax the one percent."[12] Since 1970, total federal taxes on the general population are basically unchanged at about 23 percent of total income. But for the richest, federal taxes have fallen by half, from 70 percent to 35 percent.[13] This has been referred to as "trickle down" economics—the belief that if the rich are taxed less, the economy will grow and generate jobs and economic gains for everyone. But the economy has not grown well.

The combination of declining federal taxes on the rich and rising incomes at the top has tempted a number of U.S. states to adopt so-called millionaire taxes on top incomes. States have been, in essence, going where the money is to find new revenues at the top of the income distribution. Since the early 2000s, states including New Jersey, California, Maryland, New York, Wisconsin, Oregon, and Connecticut have adopted additional tax brackets for the very highest income earners. Several other states, including Washington and Illinois, have tried to pass such taxes and failed. A central question, in all of these political campaigns, has been whether these blue state policies show leadership in addressing inequality—by drafting a new social contract with the rich—or whether the rich will simply migrate to red states that offer lower tax rates.

There are growing signs that the elites themselves are troubled by rising inequality and may be more tolerant of higher taxes than the current political discourse suggests. Some of the richest people in America—Bill Gates and Warren Buffett—have led a campaign for the Giving Pledge, calling on fellow billionaires to give away at least half their wealth to charitable causes. Many have signed on. As Buffett has said, "If you're in the luckiest 1 percent of humanity, you owe it to the rest of humanity to think about the other 99 percent."[14] Buffett also offered a longer justification for the Giving Pledge, rooted in the idiosyncrasy of market income:

> I've worked in an economy that rewards someone who saves the lives of others on a battlefield with a medal, rewards a great teacher with thank-you notes from parents, but rewards those who can detect the mispricing of securities with sums reaching into the billions.[15]

This comes from the spirit of *noblesse oblige*—a feeling among those at the top that they have not only amassed a great fortune but have also been very fortunate.

What about the less elite millionaires like top doctors, lawyers, and business managers? Do they feel a similar sense of obligation that comes with their more modest fortunes? Concern about inequality often comes from a more personal place for higher-end income earners: parental responsibility and concern about how their children will fare in a winner-take-all society. Sociologist Marianne Cooper spent years interviewing rich and poor families in Silicon Valley.[16] Poor families, she found, rarely talked to her about the macro-economy or trends in inequality; they were focused on making ends meet week to week. But high-income families were keenly aware of growing economic polarization. This drove an intense concern about their children, a fear that as parents they were not doing enough to prepare them for an increasingly unequal world and a worry that they had not yet saved enough to pay for their kids' master's degrees. High-income families saw a world split between the haves and the have-nots as an existential concern for their children, and this framed much of their own self-doubts as parents. This is an intergenerational Rawlsian "veil of ignorance": The successful worry about inequality because they do not know where their children will end up in the economic world of tomorrow.

Is this enough for top income earners to see progressive taxation as legitimate? In some ways, inequality may push people at the top to even more preciously guard their income. The top 1 percent may well alternate between feeling some *noblesse oblige* on one hand, yet also feeling some resentment that taxes are getting in the way of their responsibility to their children. While people at the top may genuinely wish the country was less economically polarized, they also know there is an arms race at play.

So, politically, there is room for appeals to the nobler instincts of top income earners. Following Warren Buffett's lead, the Patriotic Millionaires activist group has been cajoling their fellow rich to accept greater tax responsibility. The Patriotic Millionaires say they reject the idea that

> only a very small group of highly talented elites is responsible for creating the wealth. . . . We [millionaires] have been the biggest beneficiaries of this system called America, and we should pay more to keep it running. We have reaped the greatest share of the benefits. We should contribute the largest portion of the investment.[17]

In 2011, a survey of millionaire investors by the investment group Spectrem found that a sizable majority (67 percent) supported higher taxes on millionaires.[18]

Nevertheless, many of the rich are fiercely opposed to higher taxes. A political movement led by activist Grover Norquist has made low income tax rates perhaps the deepest and most profound commitment held by the Republican Party.[19] Some political and social scientists have suggested that, in the modern era, millionaire taxes may be simply too contentious and polarizing to be viable tax policy and that future revenue needs should probably be met with sales taxes.[20] But these questions are ultimately normative: Which kind of tax system is genuinely seen as fairer and closer to the moral beliefs of most Americans? Millionaire taxes can be seen as penalizing the hardest-working and most productive members of society, and thus as an affront to American work ethic values. On the other hand, millionaire taxes can been seen as calling for the largest tax contributions from those who benefit the most from American capitalism and from the protections and rights of the U.S. Constitution. However, in many political debates today, these crucial conversations about fairness and moral values are often sidestepped. Economists like Martin Feldstein and his political proponents argue, in essence, that the morality or fairness of the tax code is irrelevant: Millionaire taxes are simply self-defeating because the rich will leave.

If millionaires are voting with their feet—and moving to the tax systems that they want—what kinds of tax plans can survive this pressure? If there is a great deal of millionaire tax migration, perhaps questions of fairness really are just idle discussions of unworkable aspirations.

This raises the central question of this book. Can different places sustain different tax rates on the rich? Texas will never want to be a state that taxes millionaires at a higher rate. Internationally, some countries are deeply committed to tax systems with low rates on the rich. If a "global tax on wealth"— as Thomas Piketty advocates—is impossible, how much room is left for national policymaking and varieties of elite taxation?

This book takes on some broad intellectual territory. It might be seen as the demography of the rich—the migration of millionaires and billionaires—with a focus on the geographic limits and possibilities of taxation. But deep at the center of this inquiry is the importance of *place* in the modern world. I argue that place remains centrally important to the lives and incomes of the rich in the United States and abroad. Globalization and migration have been misunderstood for many years. And this has important implications for how we think about taxation and geographic mobility.

Sociologist Saskia Sassen writes that globalization is not just a process of global dispersion, but also one of spatial concentration. Globalization is seen in offshoring factories and jobs around the world, building global networks of franchises and subsidiaries, and the rise of international financial markets to facilitate worldwide investment and payments. But alongside this has been a corresponding growth of "headquarter work": the coordination and management of these increasingly complex businesses. The "top-level financial, legal, accounting, managerial, executive and planning functions," Sassen notes, have not been globalized but are actually more geographically concentrated.[21] Global production systems are managed by elite workers in New York, Chicago, and Los Angeles, and internationally, in London, Paris, and Hong Kong. The corporate services complex—made up of the top firms in law, accounting, management consulting, and investment banking—is overwhelmingly concentrated in the major cities of wealthy countries. Globalization has not meant that elite professionals and the executive class can now live wherever they wish. On the contrary, place is more important than ever, and top income earners are more and more concentrated in major cities like New York.

While domestic and international travel have increased dramatically in this latest era of globalization, actual migration—moving one's home and life to a different place—has changed very little, especially for people born in the rich countries of the OECD (Organisation for Economic Cooperation and Development). Understanding how place still matters in a globalized world is important not just for the design of tax policy, and not just for millionaires, but for how we all understand our lives and the ties that bind us to where we live.

Data and Methods

How does one study the geographic mobility patterns of the highest income earners? My initial entry point into this research area was in studying the effect of a so-called millionaire tax passed in New Jersey in 2004. This policy raised the marginal tax rate on incomes above $500,000 by 2.6 percentage points. There were widespread criticisms, however, that the tax was causing rich New Jerseyans to leave the state. To study the effects of this tax, the New Jersey Division of Taxation granted me and my colleagues unique access to the complete NJ-1040 tax records for the years 2000 to 2007.[22] This provided a virtual census of high income earners, with information on income, taxes paid, and whether a tax filer entered or exited the state.

These administrative tax data solved a central problem in the study of economic elites: the difficulty of acquiring good data on them. Millionaires tend to be protective of their privacy and reluctant to participate in interviews or surveys. By definition, elites are few in number and hard to find using conventional random-sample survey methods. The U.S. Census Bureau— which has very big data on the population—"topcodes" income data so that the highest earners cannot be analyzed for confidentiality reasons. All of this means that most of what is known about millionaires is largely anecdotal and speculation. The New Jersey tax data allowed us to conduct the first study using actual migration data for the very highest income earners.[23]

For this book, I drew on special access to the tax returns of every million-dollar income earner in every U.S. state over thirteen years. This information includes 45 million tax records from anyone who ever filed a tax return with annual income of at least $1 million between the years 1999 and 2011. Access to these data is provided through collaboration with researchers at the Office for Tax Analysis at the U.S. Department of the Treasury.[24] These big administrative data provide, in essence, a census of top income earners in the United States, with data on how much they make, where they live, and where they move. This is an extraordinary database from which to probe central questions about the mobility of the rich.

The term "millionaire" often refers to individuals with high net worth: those with $1 million or more in financial assets. The focus here is even more exclusive: This is primarily a study of people who can make that amount in a single year. I focus on income earners rather than net wealth because income is subject to taxation in the United States whereas wealth per se is generally not. Thus, "millionaires" in this study—those making at least $1 million in annual income—are more elite than the 1 percent. They represent roughly the top 0.3 percent of people in the income distribution. As a group, their median income is $1.7 million. Some—about 4 percent of the group—make at least $10 million per year.

I also examine international data on people with extremely high net worth—those on the Forbes list of the world's billionaires. Admittedly, this is a shift from big data to small data: Only about 1,000 people appear on the Forbes list in 2010, the year on which I focus. The Americans on this list are all likely included in the millionaire set I draw from IRS tax returns. But those on the Forbes list can be identified by name, and they make an interesting subset of people who have high annual income, as well as the greatest amounts of accumulated wealth. More importantly, the Forbes billionaire data allow me to look at the international migration of the richest in the world—the propensity of economic elites from any country to move to lower-tax countries. This gives us multiple angles on the mobility of the super-rich: all high income earners in the United States, the 400 Americans with the most extreme wealth, and the 1,000 richest people worldwide.

Finally, I delve into the world of global finance and international tax havens. If the rich can readily hide their money in offshore accounts, this could provide an alternative to tax-motivated migration. Rather than moving to avoid taxes, perhaps they can simply move their money. The Panama Papers leak showed the use of anonymous shell companies to conceal the identity of powerful and wealthy people around the world. I examine how the offshore economy works, how much financial wealth is hidden offshore, and roughly how much tax evasion is occurring through these accounts. This examination complements the core analysis of the mobility of millionaires with a look at the movement of their money.

. . .

The central argument of this book unfolds in three chapters. In Chapter 2 I present comprehensive evidence on millionaire migration within the United States. I draw on 45 million tax records from every million-dollar income earner in every U.S. state over thirteen years, tracking the place from which millionaires file their taxes. I present a series of tests of whether top earners are better seen as "mobile millionaires" or "embedded elites." This provides a demographic analysis of the rich in America. I analyze how often millionaires migrate and how often they move to lower-tax states. I also examine—along states' narrow border regions and in cities that cross state lines—whether millionaires cluster on the lower tax side of the border. The chapter also draws on the Forbes 400 list of richest Americans, to explore whether the super-rich are drawn to low-tax states. I supplement this with U.S. Census data to reveal striking patterns in migration by age and education over the life course.

Chapter 3 then zooms out to the global landscape. At the global level, millionaire tax flight could mean the movement of top earners and their families, or it could mean simply the movement of money through shell companies and foreign bank accounts. This chapter explores both possibilities. In terms of global mobility, how many of the world's billionaires live outside their country of birth? How many reside in the world's well-known tax havens? The chapter builds on the numbers and the life trajectories of the world's billionaires to understand what drives the global migration of the super-rich. Moreover, the international tax game is not just about the migration of people. I explore new research on the enormous sums of money held in offshore tax havens, an issue highlighted in leaks from the Panama Papers. The offshoring of money is, to some degree, a substitute for offshoring one's life. I examine the extent to which elites can use offshore accounts to evade taxes and whether a careful structuring of shell companies can be a substitute for actually moving to an offshore tax haven. As it turns out, offshoring personal financial wealth accomplishes less tax evasion than one might think.

Chapter 4 takes a step back to reflect more deeply on millionaire migration and why it is not more common in the modern world. This chapter is about understanding why place is important and why mobility—especially for those at the top—is less appealing than we often think. I emphasize that human capital—knowledge, skills, and abilities—tends to be place-specific. For example, top-level financial analysts have place-specific human capital. Their skills will be most valued in a handful of major cities that specialize in finance, which limits where they can live. Similarly, social capital depends on living in the place where people have their best social contacts and connections. And cultural capital means taking advantage of opportunities where people have their strongest cultural fit. The place-specific nature of these forms of capital grows over time, especially as people advance in their careers. By the time people reach the peak of their careers—and enter the top tax brackets of their states and countries—many have become embedded elites. Even if the world's borders are open to them, their economic advantages are strongest in the places where they built their careers. Moving at one's peak career stage is rare because so much human, social, and cultural capital has already been vested in one's location. Places are sticky: When you achieve success in a place, it becomes harder to leave.

I conclude the fourth chapter on a broad note about globalization and the nation-state. It is tempting to think that without legal borders and citizenship rules, populations would readily spill across borders. But, at least among people born in rich countries, national borders are much less important than we think. Countries are held together mostly by the gravity of home-field advantage and place-specific capital. If the countries of the Western world dissolved their shared borders, it is unlikely that many people would move. What borders mostly do, we will see, is keep people out—specifically people born in the global South: These are the developing countries in Asia, Africa, and Latin America, and people from these regions would have a much higher standard of living if they could work in a rich Western country. For people born in rich countries, no such opportunity differentials motivate systematic migration, and plenty of place-specific capital deters it. Among rich countries themselves, few citizens have much reason to live elsewhere—even if the legal borders were completely open.

In the final chapter, I focus on the policy implications emerging from this research on millionaire migration and the taxation of the rich. What should be the policy priorities of places that seek to address inequality and build a foundation for shared prosperity without setting off the migration of top income earners? The threat of millionaire migration does limit the ability of states to set higher tax rates for the rich but by less than one might think. I suggest a modest agenda for addressing individual tax evasion through offshore shell companies. And finally, I conclude by suggesting that it may be better for places to compete for young, highly educated individuals who are just beginning their careers, rather than trying to attract the late-career individuals who currently have the highest incomes.

Now, let's start exploring the evidence and see what mobility looks like for millionaires in the United States.

Do the Rich Flee High Taxes? 2

Hedge fund manager David Tepper—one of the richest people in America—relocated from New Jersey to Florida in 2016. In doing so, he reignited a heated debate about tax flight among the rich. While Tepper did not publicly discuss his reasons for moving, many commentators attributed it to New Jersey's millionaire tax. Indeed, his move seemed to confirm the simple economics conveyed in Governor Chris Christie's warning: "If you tax them, they will leave."[1]

Internationally, there have been high-profile occasions of tax flight. In 2013, French actor Gerard Depardieu renounced his citizenship and moved to Russia to avoid France's high tax burden. At the time, Russia's deputy prime minister boasted about his country's 13 percent flat income tax. "The West," he said, "has an especially poor knowledge of our tax system. When they learn about it, we expect a mass migration of wealthy Europeans to Russia."[2]

Are these anecdotes capturing an important reality of the elite today? Do millionaires migrate more often than the rest of us? Or are we searching for confirmation of wrongheaded assumptions about elites and globalization? It seems obvious that millionaires *travel* more often than the general public—travel is a classic luxury good. But business travel and vacationing are very different from moving one's home and life to a new state. To what extent do top income earners migrate away from places with high income taxes?

From one perspective, we can think of top income earners as "mobile millionaires" who are searching for the lowest tax places to live. The rich have the resources to move, and they have marketable skills that could be valued in many different places. Indeed, most Americans see the rich as different from ordinary folks. In surveys, they say the rich are intelligent and hardworking but also greedy and less honest.[3] Tax migration fits easily into this framework, suggesting a kind of astute-but-detached calculating nature, an acquisitive drive that supersedes social bonds and emotional ties to home.

Such views of the rich may well be accurate. But the alternative perspective is to think of the rich as "embedded elites" who have little need or interest in moving away from places where they are highly successful. Migration may be less about personality and more about circumstance. People move not because they are cold and calculating but because of where their opportunities lie. By definition, elites are at the top of their game. They have become very successful in the place where they live: In many cases, they have become deeply embedded insiders, rich not only in income but also in personal connections and social capital. Often, they are late-career professionals and past the age or life-cycle stage when one is likely to move. They have ascended to the top of the income hierarchy, which pushes them into a high tax bracket but also signals high-level insider status. The incentive for such individuals to move elsewhere is unclear at best.

Which view of the rich is more accurate? Are the rich mobile millionaires or embedded elites? Answering this question will help us determine appropriate tax policies for elites: Should states and countries have higher or lower millionaire taxes? If the rich are highly mobile, it may not be realistic to have millionaire taxes. However, if the rich are embedded elites, higher tax rates on million-dollar incomes are more viable.

·   ·   ·

One of the biggest challenges in studying millionaires is getting reliable data on them: Those at the top are hard to reach, and they do not tend to respond to social surveys. A group of political scientists commented on the challenges of interviewing millionaires: "It is extremely difficult to make personal contact with wealthy Americans. Most of them are very busy. Most zealously protect their privacy. They often surround themselves with professional gatekeepers whose job it is to fend off people like us."[4] After extensive efforts using experienced hired staff, they were able to interview only 83 millionaires in Chicago for their study.

This chapter takes a different strategy. I use big data from administrative tax records. Millionaires must file taxes, and this provides census-scale data on their income and where they live. I analyze restricted IRS data on the tax returns filed by all million-dollar income earners in every state, over the thirteen years of 1999 to 2011. The data set includes 45 million de-identified tax records on high income earners. These are the federal tax returns of every high-income individual in the country, showing where millionaires live and where they move. The data were anonymized so it was not possible to look up and see, for example, who is taxpayer number 8498251. But every person's tax returns were tracked over time, showing where the person lived over the thirteen-year time period.[5] People who moved—that is, changed the state from which they file their federal taxes—in a year when they earned $1 million or more are labeled "millionaire migrants."

In a typical year, about 500,000 people earn at least $1 million in income. This group is more exclusive than the 1 percent—specifically, they are the 0.3 percent. On average, they earn about $1.7 million in a year—roughly 32 times the median household income. The term "millionaire" often connotes accumulated wealth, but these data refer to annual incomes—people who make more in one year than what many people ever accumulate over their lifetime.[6]

With these data, we can probe a series of questions that follow from the mobile millionaire versus the embedded elite hypotheses. First, do top income earners tend to live in low-tax states? Second, are they highly mobile—do they show high rates of migration? And third, when millionaires move, do they tend to gravitate toward states with lower taxes on the rich? Answering these questions will give clear insight into whether millionaires should be thought of as mobile or embedded.

State Tax Systems: Soaking the Rich or Taxing the Poor?

The defining feature of a state tax system is the balance between sales tax and income tax. Sales tax is regressive, placing a higher tax burden on lower income earners. The income tax is progressive, so that the tax rate rises with economic success. States have different mixes of these two types of taxation, which have differential effects on different social classes.[7]

A sales tax is regressive due to two compounding factors. First, the sales tax is nominally a flat tax. The tax rate is the same whether you are buying bread or buying a Bentley: Luxuries are taxed at the same rate as necessities. Second, the sales tax applies only to income that is spent on consumption. In principle, this provides a good incentive: People can avoid taxation by saving or investing more of their income, which is both good for personal finances and good for the economy (unless we are in a recession). In practice, however, it is much harder for the poor to save than it is for the rich. The poor typically spend all of their income each year, whereas top earners are often able to save a substantial portion of their earnings.

In a world without economic hardship, the sales tax would make a lot of sense. It is easy to administer. It is a relatively invisible tax: We pay a little bit of it each time we buy something we want, and we do not file an annual report documenting how much we paid in total. And a sales/consumption tax seems to help encourage saving. But in our world where people's ability to save is very uneven, the sales tax introduces significant economic unfairness.

The gasoline tax is a case in point. Gasoline is a pollutant for our environment, so it should be taxed simply to discourage gas-guzzling SUVs and long commutes. But fuel consumption does not vary much by income level. Households typically spend about $3,000 a year on gasoline.[8] Fuel consumption does of course rise with income, but the difference between the top and the bottom income earners is not large.[9] There is only so much gas a rich person can use. This means gasoline taxes are a much larger part of poor people's budgets than they are of rich people's budgets.

So it is with sales taxes in general. Across the country, the poor typically pay about 7 percent of their income in sales and excise taxes. But top income earners pay only about 1 percent of their income toward such taxes.[10] This makes life harder for lower income earners. States that rely on sales taxes are making low- and middle-income families pay for a much larger share of the overall cost of running the state.

Income taxes are central to balancing out the unfairness of the sales tax. The poor pay almost nothing in state income taxes (0.2 percent), whereas average top earners pay about 4 percent of their total budget in state income taxes.[11] Indeed, high income earners contribute a large portion of the revenues generated from state income tax. But although state income taxes are progressive, they do not fully balance out sales taxes, because sales taxes tend to generate more revenue. In every state, the poor pay a greater share of their budgets in state and local taxes than do the rich. Part of why the poor are struggling is because "the state and local taxes they face make them even poorer," as Kathy Newman and Rourke O'Brien document in their book *Taxing the Poor.*[12]

In essence, all state tax systems are regressive. But states that rely more on income taxes come the closest to tax fairness. In California, for example, the rich pay about 7.5 percent of their budgets in state and local taxes—mostly through the income tax. Lower income Californians pay about 10 percent of their budget in tax but mostly through the sales tax. The tax disparity is about 2.5 percentage points—one of the smallest in the country. Florida provides a stark contrast: The poor pay about 12 percent of their income in state and local taxes, while the rich pay only 2 percent. Washington State has the most unequal tax burden in the country: The poor pay a 17 percent overall tax rate, whereas top income earners pay less than 3 percent. This is the result of a system of high sales tax combined with no state income tax.[13]

Millionaire taxes are often derided as "soak the rich" tax policies. However, state tax systems infringe on the incomes and standard of living of the poor much more than for the well-to-do. As a share of people's incomes, existing state tax systems impact the poor and the middle class much more than the rich. At the state level, "soak the rich" income taxes are more about balancing out the regressive features of the sales tax. State millionaire taxes, if feasible, could make significant progress in restoring fairness to the state tax systems, while helping to alleviate inequality. This is why it is so important to investigate the implications of these taxes.

The decentralized American political system means that some states have adopted much more progressive tax systems than others. At the same time, the United States can be thought of as a world composed of fifty-one small open economies with free migration between them. Can states sustain taxation on the rich when other nearby states have no income tax at all? How sustainable are these varieties of elite taxation in the United States?

Where Do the Highest Income Earners Live?

By and large, the different tax systems at the state level have been in place for a long time. Most state income taxes were originally adopted in the 1960s and 1970s.[14] The last major state tax reform occurred in 1991, when Connecticut shifted from being a relative tax haven to adopting a progressive income tax. Of course, there have been many smaller changes since then, but the relative ranking of high- and low-tax states for top income earners has not changed much in the past three decades. If millionaires are strongly motivated to live in states that minimize their tax burden, they have had generations to make it happen.

So, the first and most basic test of the mobile millionaire hypothesis examines whether millionaires are especially concentrated in low-tax states. The average state has 1.4 millionaires for every 1,000 residents. The highest millionaire concentration is in Connecticut, with 4.4 per 1,000 population. Filling out the top five states/districts are the District of Columbia (3.6), New York (3.0), New Jersey (2.8), and Massachusetts (2.7). Elite income earners are heavily concentrated in the mid-Atlantic region, particularly along the "BosWash corridor." These are also generally high-tax states for top income earners. Nevertheless, some low-tax states, such as Florida and Nevada, also have above-average millionaire concentrations (both 2.0).

Figure 2.1 shows millionaire concentrations for every state, compared to the income tax rate on top earners. The left side of the figure shows the states with zero income tax. Millionaire density in these states ranges from 1.0 per 1,000 people in Tennessee to 2.0 in Florida; as a group, the zero-tax states have about average concentrations of millionaires. As we move rightward in the graph, we see states with higher and higher tax rates on the rich. Millionaire concentration inches up slightly as the tax rate rises. This is especially clear for New York, New Jersey, and California, which are high-tax states with a high concentration of millionaires.

Millionaires are not any more likely to live in states with low or no income taxes (such as Texas or Florida) than in states with high income taxes (such as New Jersey or California). Millionaires in America are more or less evenly distributed among high- and low-tax states, and they do not show a clear preference for one or the other.

Millionaires per 1,000 residents

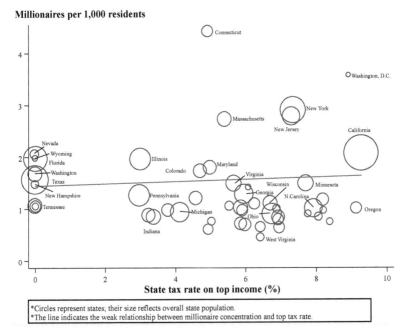

*Circles represent states; their size reflects overall state population.
*The line indicates the weak relationship between millionaire concentration and top tax rate.

Figure 2.1. Millionaire Concentration and Top State Tax Rates, 1999 to 2011. States are weighted by overall population as indicated by circle size (i.e., California is the largest circle because it has the largest overall population). The states on the left are zero-tax states; states shown toward the right have increasingly higher tax rates on the rich. The tax rate is the effective income tax rate on a representative millionaire (earning $1.7 million per year). The line shows the weak relationship between millionaire concentration and top tax rate (the slope of the linear regression). Sources: U.S. Department of the Treasury, IRS microdata (N = 45 million) and the NBER TAXSIM program. Adapted from Young et al. (2016).

Millionaire Migration

"There is nothing more portable," a California Senate leader once said, "than a millionaire and his money."[15] This is the notion of a jet-set elite, for whom place is fluid and fungible; this group can readily change their location when need or advantage calls for it. As it turns out, these notions are completely wrong.

The rate of migration among millionaires is low. Millionaires move less often than the general public and much less often than the poor. Figure 2.2

shows annual migration by income level, starting with the left side (the very lowest incomes) and moving to the right for people earning millions per year. The highest migration rates are among low income earners. People making only about $10,000 per year have a 4.5 percent migration rate. These folks are struggling, and migration seems to be part of their survival strategy and their search for work. People are more likely to move when things are not working out for them where they live. Low income earners move almost twice as often as millionaires.

In general, migration declines steadily as income rises. The least mobile people are those earning about $100,000, who have a 2 percent migration rate. The intuition that top income earners are very mobile is simply wrong. For the general population, the migration rate is 2.9 percent. For millionaires, the migration rate is only 2.4 percent.

There is, however, some truth in the mobile millionaire hypothesis. Above $100,000 in annual income, migration does begin to inch back upward. At

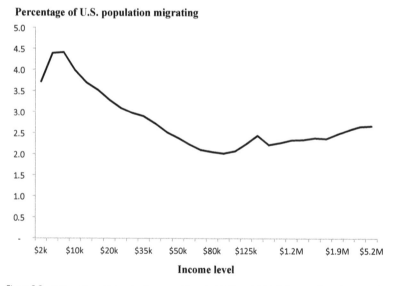

Percentage of U.S. population migrating

Income level

Figure 2.2. Migration Rates by Income Level, 1999 to 2011. The graph indicates that migration declines as people earn higher incomes. Sources: U.S. Department of the Treasury, IRS microdata, 1 percent sample of all tax filers (N = 24 million) and 100 percent sample of people making $1 million or more (N = 45 million). Adapted from Young et al. (2016).

best, one can say that millionaires are more residentially mobile than the upper middle class. But even people making over $5 million per year (the last data point in Figure 2.2) have a migration rate of 2.7 percent—still lower than the population average and much lower than the rate among the poor.

We tend to think of mobility—the ability to live wherever one wishes—as a form of freedom and one of the privileges enjoyed by the rich. Mobility and migration are ingrained ideals in U.S. culture, fitting in with the belief that the rich are more geographically mobile than the poor. It has been said that "to move, to change—that is what enjoys prestige, as against stability, which is often synonymous with inaction."[16] Despite its evocative resonance with ideals of freedom, interstate migration has been declining for decades.[17] If this kind of mobility is freedom, then that freedom has been fading in America, especially for the rich.

The fact that the poor have the highest migration rates should challenge these understandings of migration. Migration is mostly about people who are struggling to find opportunities, not those who are cashing in on their success. *Travel* and *migration* are very different things, and they are done by different social classes. Jet-setting around Europe and Asia is a luxury good that is largely restricted to families of considerable means. Migration, in contrast, means uprooting one's life and restarting in a new place, and it is much more common among the poor. Conflating actual migration with business and leisure travel has led to mistaken assumptions about the migration rates of millionaires.

Tax-Induced Migration

The rate of millionaire migration is low. However, when millionaires do move, how often are they moving specifically for tax purposes? How can we tell if a move is motivated by tax avoidance? In practice, this is a difficult question, because people's internal motivations are hard to observe. But, the first criterion is that the move must be from a higher tax to a lower tax state. If a move does not save on taxes—or indeed, if it *increases* taxes—it cannot be called "tax migration."

Do millionaires ever move into states that charge them higher income taxes? Yes. In fact, this is very common. Some 32 percent of millionaire migrations in our data were moves to a state that charged the individuals a higher income tax rate than where they came from. Each of these moves contradicts the notion of tax-induced migration—they are moves that happened *despite* the tax hit involved. An additional 21 percent of moves were tax neutral—moves between states with essentially the same tax rate.[18] This reinforces the idea that millionaires often move for reasons unrelated to taxes. Finally, the remaining 47 percent of migrations were toward a state with a lower tax rate on elites, so that the mover had a lower tax rate after the move. These are the moves that provide evidence of tax-motivated migration.

Overall, these data give some fairly clear evidence of tax motivation in millionaire migration: The rich are more likely to move to places that charge them lower taxes (47 percent) than to places that charge them higher taxes (32 percent). The difference between these flows (47 percent versus 32 percent) shows the "excess" migration from high- to low-tax states, which amounts to 15 percent of migrations. In other words, about 15 percent of millionaire migrations on balance appear to have a tax motivation and provide a tax advantage.

Elsewhere, my coauthors and I have published much more sophisticated and detailed statistical analysis for readers wanting to wade through multiple levels of scientific rigor. However, the simple analysis shown above gives a good representation of what is found with more advanced methods. The more complex models analyze flows of millionaires from each one of the fifty states and the District of Columbia into every other state. These analyses use so-called gravity models to look at migration flows between 2,550 possible state pairings—such New York to Florida, New York to South Carolina, New York to Illinois, and so on for every state pair and in both directions. The results show a statistically significant effect of millionaires gravitating toward states with lower tax rates on top incomes. The effect is modest in size but robust across many different model specifications and different subgroups of millionaires.

For example, do the conclusions change if we take into account other tax rates that are important for state revenues, such as the sales tax or the property tax? What if a state has an inheritance tax? What if we consider how migration is affected by the economic prosperity of states, taking into account state unemployment rates and average incomes? What if we account for the natural climate, measured by winter temperatures? Perhaps most importantly, what if we consider the price of residential land, which captures the desirability of residing in a state? All of these are good questions, but none of these factors changes the basic conclusion that millionaires are prone to move to lower tax states. Taken together, these control variables actually make that conclusion a bit stronger.

The conclusion also is much the same for super-elite earners making at least $10 million per year. It is the same for millionaires who own businesses and for those who mostly live off capital gains. The most important difference, however, is that among the general population, taxes do *not* affect migration patterns. Top income earners are more motivated than the general public to find a lower-tax place to live.

It is clear from these data that tax migration among millionaires is occurring. How large is the effect? What kind of impact does this have on the geography of the elite in America?

The overall millionaire migration rate is low: 2.4 percent. Further, only a small portion of these moves—15 percent—bring a net tax advantage. Overall *tax migration* among millionaires is thus a small fraction out of a small fraction: 15 percent of 2.4 percent. Only 0.3 percent of the overall millionaire population, on balance, shifted to a lower tax state.

Let's put this in more concrete terms. Over thirteen years, there were about 135,000 millionaire migrations in America. The net movement of millionaires into lower tax states during the years 1999 to 2011 amounts to about 20,000 millionaires. However, this is from a population of 3.7 million people who collectively filed 45 million annual tax returns during this time. Tax-induced movements represent a vanishingly small share of the millionaire population.

There is a grain of truth in concerns about millionaire tax flight. When millionaires do migrate, they are more likely to move to a state with a lower tax rate. However, the effect is small and has little impact on a state's overall stock of millionaires.[19]

The Florida Effect

One of the most striking facts about tax migration is that, if we temporarily set aside migration between Florida and other states, the evidence for tax migration virtually disappears. The reasons for this are intriguing.

Florida has a lot of millionaire migration. About 30 percent of all millionaire migrations in the United States involve Florida: Roughly 20 percent are top earners moving to Florida, and another 10 percent are top earners leaving Florida. Virtually every state in the country, but especially New York and New Jersey, sees at least some net migration of its top earners into the state. Florida does not create many of its own millionaires, and without these inflows it would have a declining millionaire population. But vibrant millionaire inflows are having a big influence on the state.

Setting aside migrations in and out of Florida, it is almost equally likely that a millionaire will move to a state with a higher tax rate as a lower tax rate: 35 percent of moves are to higher tax states, 38 percent are to lower tax states. The 3-percentage point difference is negligible, demonstrating that there is little interest among millionaires in the tax difference between "sending" and "receiving" states. (The remaining 27 percent of moves are between states with roughly the same tax rate.)

This is important because, in the business of offering low-tax rates to millionaires, Florida has at least six real competitors: Texas, Tennessee, New Hampshire, Nevada, Wyoming, and Washington. All of these states have the same zero income tax rate as Florida. Florida is not the only state with no income tax on the rich, but it is the only state that seems to achieve tax haven status. Why are these other states unable to systematically attract the rich from high-tax states?

It could be that Florida simply has a monopoly on tax haven status in the United States. If high income earners wish to avoid paying state income tax, they simply move to Florida rather than to any of its low-tax competitors. Other options are nice, but one tax haven is good enough. Indeed, tax havens might be natural monopolies, because place is a network good. If millionaires like to live in places that have other millionaires, one tax haven state might become a focus of tacit coordination and become *the* place to go.

By analogy, with social media, almost everyone uses Facebook rather than Myspace or any other comparable website, because almost everyone else is on Facebook. Facebook is a natural monopoly because people need only one social networking site, and it works best to have everyone on the same site. Similarly, if millionaires want to be around other high-status people and want to enjoy similar kinds of expensive amenities, such as golf courses and fine-dining establishments, tax havens might be most appealing when most millionaires all go to the same place. In this sense, there is nothing surprising about Florida's unique status as a magnate for millionaire migration: It is better for millionaires if there is just one good tax haven on which they can all converge.

At the same time, Florida is unique in a number of ways that are unrelated to taxes. It is the only state with coastal access to the Caribbean Sea. Florida is the Hawaii of the East Coast, with similar amounts of warmth and sunshine. Unlike the other low-tax states, it is tremendously popular as a vacation destination and a cruise ship port. Florida is in the South, but Floridians are not Southerners, and most of the state is culturally very different from the Deep South. The city of Tampa is more like the Jersey Shore than Alabama, and many rich Florida enclaves are most comparable to the Hamptons. So, for the rich, is Florida a tax haven or a luxury resort? Does Florida migration demonstrate the benefits of maintaining a low-tax rate for the rich, or does it show the benefits of being an East Coast tropical location?

Here is the key question: If Florida had a millionaire tax rate equal to that in New York and New Jersey—from which many of its migrants come— would this break the allure of the Sunshine State? Would Texas, New Hampshire, and Wyoming become the new centers for millionaire migration? Or would a high-tax Florida continue to be the migration destination for East Coast elites? Part of Florida's migration may well fade if it became a high-tax state. But it is hard to know how much.

One of the disappointing facts about Florida is that, despite its tax haven standing, Florida is not entirely a low-tax state. The benefits of attracting millionaires have not trickled down to lower income earners—at least not in their tax bill. The state has high sales and excise taxes, which result in high-tax burdens on lower income earners. The overall effective tax rate on the poor in Florida is many times higher than that of top earners (12 percent versus 2 percent). For the poorest 20 percent of income earners, Florida has one of the highest tax rates in the country.[20]

Border Counties and Border Cities

Given the questions and doubts raised by Florida, how can we dig deeper into the millionaire data to search for evidence of tax migration? Can we test the mobile millionaire hypothesis in a way that is not skewed by Florida's tropical appeal?

The geographic borders of states offer another pathway into exploring tax migration. Border regions showcase the contrasts between different state policies, within a narrow geographic space that makes relocation easy.

The border between Oregon and Washington is the most striking example. Oregon has long had one of the most progressive income tax systems in the country. Washington State, in contrast, has never had a state income tax.[21] Oregon expects high income earners to pay much of the state's operating costs, whereas Washington relies on sales taxes that place much of the revenue burden on lower income earners. In simpler terms, Oregon taxes the rich, while Washington taxes the poor. These two tax systems meet along the banks of the Columbia River—progressive taxation sits cheek by jowl with a system of regressive taxation.

For someone on an afternoon walk, any spot along the border between Oregon and Washington might seem much like the other (Figure 2.3). If taxes are important to where high-income people live, the top earners in the Oregon border counties do not need to move to Florida: They can simply relocate to the other side of the river, staying close to home but with a potentially large tax savings. In the figure, the medium shading on the Washington side shows where rich Oregonians could move for the same tax savings as Florida's. Think of this possibility as "local" millionaire migration: It might not show up in the broader statistics of migration across all fifty states, but in these narrow border counties, do the rich tend to cluster on the low-tax side of the border?

The goal of the border-county analysis is to focus on regions where people see two counties as basically identical—except for the difference in state policies. Oregon and Washington are separated by a major river, but some seventeen bridges cross it. Mobility is easy in this border region. The geographic area is arbitrarily separated by a state line, and you can move across it with little real difference in your day-to-day life. Such a place brings the differences in state policies to the forefront: In this relatively frictionless space, people can simply cross the river for a different tax policy.

In reality, of course, it is never quite that easy. For homeowners, selling a house and buying on the other side of the river comes with big transaction

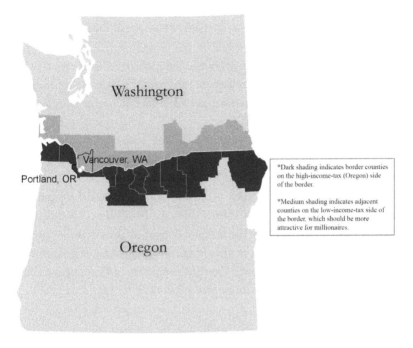

*Dark shading indicates border counties on the high-income-tax (Oregon) side of the border.

*Medium shading indicates adjacent counties on the low-income-tax side of the border, which should be more attractive for millionaires.

Figure 2.3. Border Counties of Washington and Oregon. Dark shading indicates border counties on the high-income-tax (Oregon) side of the border. Medium shading indicates adjacent counties on the low-income-tax (Washington) side of the border, which should be more attractive to millionaires. Adapted from Young et al. (2016).

costs in the form of commissions, attorneys' fees, and closing costs. Also, in most states, income is taxed where it is earned, so people would have to move both their residence and their job across the border to get the tax advantage.[22] And tax-advantageous counties are not always in commutable areas. Border counties can sometimes span long distances—in some cases, 180 miles across the Mojave Desert. Finally, people often have strong emotional attachments to their state, even when they are close to the border. For example, Vermont and New Hampshire might form a small commutable zone on the map, but residents have remarkably strong views about the state to which they belong.

These caveats aside, border regions minimize the cost of moving, and they help us focus on places that are otherwise identical except for state policies. Small geographic border regions have some sharp discontinuities in top tax rates but few obvious barriers to crossing the border. These are great places to look for the consequences of even small differences in how we tax the rich.

Within the United States, many bordering states have significant tax differences. Admittedly, tax differences are rarely as striking as at the Oregon–Washington border. But it is common to see tax differences representing 2 or 3 percent of top incomes.

Figure 2.4 maps all the counties that straddle state borders. These 1,100 counties that sit adjacent to interstate borders comprise 32 percent of the U.S. population and 35 percent of all U.S. millionaires. The darkest shading indicates counties on the high-tax side of the state border; the lightly shaded border counties are on the low-tax side. The average cross-border tax difference is 2.3 percentage points, with the sharpest differences greater than 7 points. Among the largest differences are Oregon–Washington (7.3), Vermont–New Hampshire (6.7), and North Carolina–Tennessee (6.4). Along state borders, do millionaires tend to cluster on the low-tax side of the state line?

*Light shading indicates counties on the high-tax side of state borders.

*Dark shading indicates counties on the low-tax side of state borders.

Figure 2.4. Border Counties and Tax Differences in the United States. Border counties comprise 32 percent of the U.S. population and 35 percent of all U.S. millionaires. Dark shading indicates counties on the high-tax side of state borders. Light shading indicates counties on the low-tax side. Adapted from Young et al. (2016).

These data can be analyzed in complex ways, but a simple look gives a fair impression. Between Oregon and Washington, millionaire density—the number of millionaires per thousand residents—is higher on the Oregon side. Along the Columbia River, millionaires actually tend to concentrate on the higher tax side of the border. This is striking because the tax policy differences between Oregon and Washington have, in broad form, been around as long as anyone can remember—they date back to the 1960s.[23] Generations have had time to shift the residential and business center of the border region toward the lower tax Washington side. Perhaps if there were no tax difference at the border, then *even more* millionaires would live on the Oregon side. But in the narrow geographic slice of the United States where millionaires face the single greatest tax difference at the border, they actually cluster on the high-tax side. This suggests that state income taxes are less important than we think.

Across the country, the picture we see along state borders in general is less clear. The Oregon–Washington border is a striking case study. However, in most border regions, millionaire density is higher on the side with lower taxes on elite incomes. Millionaires do tend to cluster on the low-tax side of states overall, but the difference is small and not statistically significant.

For even further granularity, we can focus on multistate cities—cities that cross a state border. As defined by the Census Bureau, the United States has 381 metropolitan areas, and 50 of these cities span at least one state border. Portland, Oregon, for example, is a border city with a significant portion of its metropolitan area across the bridge in Vancouver, Washington. Metro areas that cross state lines offer another way to look at small commutable regions that have different top taxes in different parts of the region.

In the case of Portland, the Oregon side is the growing hub of commercial and cultural life in the city, while the Washington side continues to be a sleepy, lower-middle-income suburb—despite decades of tax incentives pushing in the opposite direction. But overall, in border cities across the country, there is a small tendency for millionaire tax filers to live in the lower tax areas. Yet the difference is so small that it looks more like statistical noise than a compelling difference caused by tax rates on millionaires.

Taken together, the border county and border city analyses give weak evidence of tax migration. The findings are generally not statistically significant, and the differences are small. But the low-tax sides of state borders do tend to have a bit larger millionaire population. Taxes are clearly only one of many motivations, but this supports the argument that at least some of the millionaire migration to Florida has a tax motivation.

Billionaires in the United States

So far, we have examined location and migration for very high income earners. Billionaires, however, are a whole different class of rich. Most millionaires are the "working rich," engrossed in their professional careers and businesses and typically at the peak of their careers. For example, the chief of surgery at Massachusetts General Hospital is unlikely to move to Florida to save on taxes—that would be walking away from one of the most prestigious and best-paying positions in the country. Billionaires, on the other hand, have so definitively "made it" that surely they are free to live wherever they wish. They've already made more money than they could ever spend. Under the mobile millionaire hypothesis, billionaires should be the most mobile and the most inclined to avoid taxes.

To get a closer look at the super-rich, I turned to the Forbes 400 list of richest Americans. I started with the 2010 list and then followed their residency to 2015. Many people fall off the list by 2015, but Forbes continues to track most of them even after that. So, with the help of some hardworking research assistants, it was possible to construct a data set of the 2010 Forbes billionaires including their status in 2015. The top people on the Forbes list in 2010 were Bill Gates, Warren Buffett, Larry Ellison, Christine Walton, and the brothers Charles and David Koch. Many of the Forbes 400 billionaires own private jets, travel extensively, and own properties around the world. Still, all but five of those on the list had a clear primary residency in both years. So, where do American billionaires live? Do they tend to live in—or move to—low-tax states?

Both high-tax and low-tax states are home to America's billionaires. For instance, California is home to the highest number—92—which also has the most progressive income tax in the country. New York, too, has a steeply progressive income tax regime and can claim 70 billionaires to take the second spot on a state-level geography of riches. The next two billionaire states, however, are low-tax Texas and Florida, each with exactly 35 billionaires.

Partly, this is an unfair comparison—it is no surprise that the four largest states by population have the largest billionaire populations. But even on a per capita basis, the sizable states with the most billionaires are New York and California, followed by Florida, Wisconsin, Connecticut, Washington, and Texas.[24] In general, there is little correlation between billionaire residency and the state tax rate on top incomes. Figure 2.5 shows that the connection between billionaire population per capita and top tax rates is largely flat. There is a slight upward trend, indicating higher billionaire residency in higher tax states, but the relationship is not statistically or sociologically significant. The richest people in America seem to simply live where they want to live, with little regard to tax rates.

Billionaire mobility is also relatively low throughout these years. Among the general population, about 8 percent of Americans move across

Billionaires per million U.S. residents

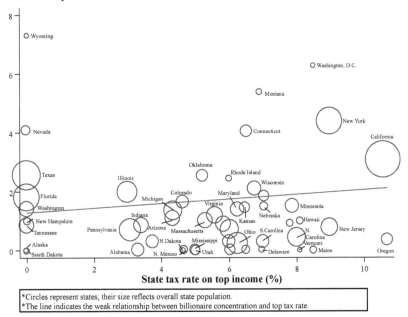

*Circles represent states; their size reflects overall state population.
*The line indicates the weak relationship between billionaire concentration and top tax rate.

Figure 2.5. Forbes Billionaire Population Per Capita, by Top State Income Tax Rate, 2010. States are weighted by overall population as indicated by circle size. The relatively flat line indicates little relationship between income and state tax rate; that is, rich people in the United States simply live where they want to live, regardless of tax rates. Sources: Forbes 400 Richest Americans (2010) and the NBER TAXSIM program.

state lines over a five-year period.[25] Among the 2010 cohort of billionaires, only 6 percent moved (22 billionaires moved between 2010 and 2015). Note that 7 percent of the 2010 billionaires had died by 2015: Billionaires are more likely to die than to move from their primary residence.

Two additional points are important here. First, when billionaires move, it is typically to Florida. Of the 22 billionaires who moved, 10 (45 percent) relocated to the Sunshine State. No billionaires moved out of Florida. Some billionaires moved into states with a higher tax rate. Oprah Winfrey, for example, moved from Illinois to California, which clearly raised her income tax rate. But overall, the few billionaire moves that occur are strongly skewed toward the lower taxation in Florida.

Second, this time period—2010 to 2015—saw the biggest increase in a state millionaire tax in the United States in three decades. In California, Proposition 30 raised the millionaire tax rate by 3 percentage points—topping out at 13.3 percent—and pushed the boundary of elite taxation by state governments to new levels. The top rate in California was now higher than any time since World War II. Skeptics loudly warned about out-migration of the rich. Yet California saw no loss in its billionaires after the tax hike. None of the Forbes 400 migrated out of California, and the state went from having 84 to 92 of the Forbes 400 by 2015. Of course, the booming tech economy drove the growth in billionaires. But the new "tax on success" did not seem to hamper the state's economy or nudge out its most successful residents.

The Forbes list offers a compelling way to compare the millionaire tax data with public information on American billionaires. The billionaire data give greater confidence in what we learned from millionaires: The superrich are spread more or less evenly across the country; they are not at all concentrated in low-tax states; and they have low migration rates, but when they do move, they have a fondness for Florida.

Why Millionaires Stay: The Demography of the Rich

Why is there so little migration among millionaires? How has the conventional wisdom—that the rich have exceptional mobility—gotten this so wrong? What social and economic factors might explain why the rich are embedded in their states?

In 2009, Facebook cofounder Eduardo Saverin moved from Florida to Singapore. He renounced his American citizenship about five months before Facebook's IPO in 2012. Estimates suggest he saved hundreds of millions in capital gains taxes. This is a bigger move than what this chapter has discussed so far—global mobility is the focus of Chapter 3—but Saverin illustrates something important about the demography of migration. Saverin was 27 years old when he moved. He was single and had no children. Saverin's shares in Facebook were worth a fortune—the company was already valued at $10 billion—but after a falling out, he no long worked at Facebook and was essentially independently wealthy. If more millionaires shared these characteristics—young, single, no children, and not working—migration would be a lot higher among the rich. All of these socioeconomic factors normally tie top income earners to the places where they live.

In the general population, marriage and children anchor people in place and make migration more difficult. Single people without children have the highest migration rates. Adding in either a spouse or children makes it harder to build consensus around a move and involves more tradeoffs. It turns out that this is no different for the rich. Both millionaires and the general population are much less likely to migrate if they are married or have children (Figure 2.6). The biggest difference is that millionaires are more likely to be married and have children. Some 90 percent of millionaires are married, compared to only 58 percent of general tax filers.

This reflects a growing social reality that, more and more, marriage has a strong income profile. In 1970, marriage rates were high and broadly similar across income levels; today there is a striking marriage gap across economic classes.[26] This is part of the reason why top earners have low migration rates. Single millionaires have a migration rate almost twice as high as married millionaires (4.1 percent and 2.2 percent, respectively). But hardly any millionaires are unmarried.

Likewise, having children in the home reduces migration rates by about one-third, regardless of one's income level. The challenge of taking kids out of school and separating them from their friends weighs on the conscience of both the rich and the poor alike. But millionaires are more likely to have children: 50 percent, compared to 40 percent among the general public. Family responsibilities are a tangible constraint on the migration of the

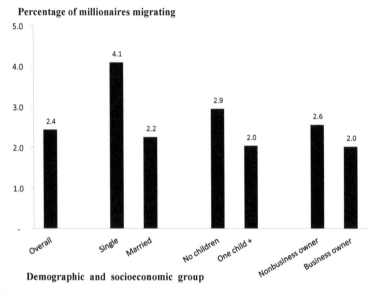

Percentage of millionaires migrating

Figure 2.6. **Millionaire Migration Rates, by Socioeconomic Group.** Millionaires are less likely to migrate if they are married, have children at home, or own a business. Source: U.S. Department of the Treasury, IRS microdata, 1999–2011 (N = 45 million). Adapted from Young et al. (2016).

rich—in similar ways as for the general public—but such responsibilities are simply more common among top income earners. In the modern age, family is one of the rewards that accrue to those with economic success. This in turn makes the wealthy less mobile.

Finally, business ownership limits migration for those at the top. Owning a business ties people to their state. Business owners are at the center of a web of socioeconomic ties—connections to their customer base, their business partners, and their employees. The reality is that, because of the complexity of these ties, bosses are less mobile than their employees. And business ownership is highly concentrated among top income earners. Some 23 percent of millionaires own a business, compared to only 4 percent of the general public.

Finally, it is important to note that millionaires are the working rich. What are the main occupations of American millionaires? The majority are either executives or managers of major businesses (42 percent) or work in finance (18 percent). A fair number are elite professionals, particularly lawyers (7 percent) and doctors (6 percent). Some 4 percent work in real estate.[27] Few of these occupations could be described as exceptionally mobile or easy to move across state lines.

Media coverage has sometimes focused on professional athletes as representative of the millionaire set. In 2013, professional golfer Phil Mickelson threatened to leave California after a new millionaire tax was passed.[28] He quickly apologized for the comments—he did not intend, apparently, to become the public face of the "bitter millionaire" movement. And, as of 2017, Mickelson still lives in California. But many PGA golfers, including Tiger Woods, live in Florida, and Woods attributes it in part to the tax rate.[29] Many top tennis players, such as the Williams sisters, also live in Florida.[30] These professional athletes are indeed the working rich, but their employer is a national and international circuit of competitions. This is an unusual type of work—even among the rich. Only 3 percent of top earners are in the combined occupational category of "sports, media, or arts." While such sports stars offer interesting anecdotes, most millionaires essentially work office jobs.

Inevitably, some occupations more easily lend themselves to geographic mobility than the average. Academia—my own profession—seems to have higher-than-average migration rates. However, it is likewise important to recognize that the combined occupational category of "professors and scientists" makes up only 1 percent of top income earners.[31]

The social demography of the rich—involving complex work commitments, business ownership, and greater family responsibilities—is part of why the rich are less mobile than the poor. However, none of these factors entirely explains the low migration among top earners. Money itself is a key factor in low migration: Economic success simply blunts the motivation to move.

The Puzzling Intersection of Education and Income

Education increases people's geographic mobility. In professional and technical fields, the job market is often national in scope. Especially for young people graduating out of top universities, the entire country is their job market, and many of them are courted by companies from all corners of the nation. This points to a fundamental puzzle: If the highly educated are very mobile, how can it be that top-level income earners have so little mobility? This puzzle holds one of the keys to the mobile millionaire versus embedded elite debate.

The tax return data I use in this chapter do not include information about education—it is not something people report on their 1040 tax forms. To look at the role of education in migration, I draw on ten years of the American Community Survey. The U.S. Census Bureau has been interviewing about 1 percent of the U.S. population each year, giving a total sample of over 24 million people over the period from 2005 to 2014. The highest income earners are topcoded, so we cannot look specifically at millionaires. But we can get an extremely detailed look at migration by age and education level for the general population.

The census data readily confirm the basic fact we learned from the tax data: The more money you make, the less likely you are to move to a different state. The poor—those making $20,000 a year—have a migration rate of 2.8 percent. Those making $200,000 a year have a migration rate of only 1.7 percent. In more detailed analyses, demographic factors like age, marital status, education, and the like do not explain away this reality: Income ties people to place.

Yet, the census data also confirm the second part of the puzzle: More education means more migration. College graduates have a migration rate of 3.2 percent—twice the rate of those who dropped out of high school (1.6 percent). This fact is also not explained away by other demographic characteristics. Higher education expands one's geographic horizon.

Hence the puzzle: Why is migration high among the best educated yet somehow low among the top earners? These two groups are typically the same people. How can they have such different migration patterns?

The divergence occurs because migration happens mostly among people who have high education but low income. At first glance, this seems like a disappointing group of individuals for whom education did not pay off. But readers with college-age children may have insight into the puzzle. Those who have *both* high education *and* low income are mostly still quite young.

Education has tremendous impact on both income and migration, but the timing of these effects could not be more different. For income, the benefits of education accrue over the course of a long career. People complete their last year of education *decades* before they earn their highest paychecks. In contrast, for geographic mobility, education has a profound impact that is close to instantaneous and very short-lived.

Figure 2.7 shows the age–migration timeline for people with different levels of education. Readers can place themselves in the graph by selecting the line that represents their highest level of education and then following the line from left to right—from age 18 to retirement. Migration rates decline over time for everyone. The differences across educational groups are dramatic—but only in the early years.

College graduates have migration rates mostly above 10 percent when they are in their 20s.[32] The parents of first-generation college students often

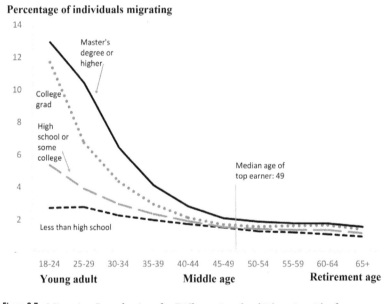

Figure 2.7. Migration Rates by Age, for Different Levels of Education. The figure shows the age–migration timeline for the general U.S. population. Migrations are across state lines. The highest point of migration is for young adults ages 18 to 24 with a master's degree or higher—most of whom are 23 to 24 years old. Migration rates decline over time for all education groups. The differences across education groups are dramatic but only when people are young. By middle age, all education groups have the same (low) rate of migration. Source: American Community Survey, 2005–2014 (N = 23 million).

worry about how education will change their families. It is a valid concern. College completion dramatically increases migration rates for young people. For people who did not complete high school, their migration rates are less than 3 percent. These two rates (10 percent versus 3 percent) reflect very different life trajectories. But there is also incredible convergence over time. If the highly educated do not migrate when they are young, the window closes very quickly. Migration rates plummet in the years after college. By age 35, roughly 80 percent of the educational difference in migration rates has been closed. By age 45, people with the most education have basically the same migration rates as people who dropped out of high school.

Migration is a young person's game. These young movers may well enter the top income brackets in the future, but they are a long way off from earning top-level incomes. If 20-somethings with advanced education were the rich in America, the mobile millionaire hypothesis surely would hold true, and state tax systems would strain under the pressure of attracting and retaining them. The reality is the opposite. By the time college graduates have a solid start in their career, the likelihood of migrating is extremely low. The burst of migration among college graduates is remarkably brief.

This life-cycle dynamic helps make sense of why millionaires have such low rates of migration. The people moving across state lines are young. But high income is a feature of the late-career stage. Of course, some young people earn extremely high incomes—such as Eduardo Saverin or his former business partner Mark Zuckerberg. But, top incomes are much more typical of the late-career stage. The median top income earner in the census data is 49 years old. In contrast, the median adult mover is 31 years old. This is a gap of almost two decades—eighteen years of life. When people move, it is typically eighteen years before they hit their peak earnings phase. People choose where to live long before they know which tax bracket life has in store for them.

The most mobile people today—those with high education but low income—are nowhere close to being in the top tax brackets of states. The mobile are not millionaires or top tax payers. By the same token, today's millionaires have low mobility, but probably many of them moved when they were young and remember the experience.

Exit Versus Voice: The Discourse of Millionaire Migration

In the classic book *Exit, Voice, and Loyalty*, social scientist Albert Hirschman highlighted voice and exit as two alternative mechanisms to produce social and economic change.[33] "Voice" is the pathway of articulating discontent and advocating for specific improvements to social conditions, workplace practices, or government policies. "Exit" is the pathway of simply leaving—shopping elsewhere, quitting a job, or moving to a different state. Advocates of tax cuts within states argue that if taxes are not reduced, millionaires will exit. This chapter has shown that exit is not an easy option for most millionaires. Millionaires, simply put, rarely leave for states with low taxes. They are too embedded in their local communities to do so. They have kids in school, they are married, they have put down roots, and they have social and business connections in their communities. Their ongoing income depends on staying in the place where they have become highly successful and have insider economic status. The threat of exit is largely empty.

Why all the talk of exit when exit is so rare? Threatening to exit makes voice powerful. By itself, voice may be ineffective for policy change if actors do not have leverage. The threat of exit provides this leverage and has become popular as a form of pressure bargaining over tax rates. Advocates of low and regressive taxes routinely assert very high mobility among the rich. When millionaire taxes are on the table, critics do not engage arguments about fairness or merit. They threaten that the rich will leave. In California, critics of the Prop 30 millionaire tax warned that "when those required to pay this tax end up leaving the state . . . they will take their tax dollars with them."[34] In Maryland, critics dubbed a millionaire tax the "Get Out of Maryland Tax Act." The situation is the same for business regulation. Dire warnings of business migration in response to state regulations rarely materialize in practice. As sociologist Bruce Carruthers and economist Naomi Lamoreaux recently concluded in their review of the business regulation literature, "businesses typically have exercised their 'voice' option more vigorously than their 'exit' option."[35]

Political discourse has spun a hypothetical world of free-floating elites who have little attachment to place and much interest in leaving for lower tax locales. This world of mobile millionaires holds a grain of truth—some millionaires do move to low-tax Florida. But top income earners in general are more like embedded elites: They are tied to place for a host of social and economic reasons, and thus are less mobile than the middle class or the poor. If states set their tax policies purely based on the risk of millionaire migration, top income tax rates would be higher in every state in the country.

Global Billionaires and International Tax Havens

3

Billionaire Migration

Global Nomads or Embedded Elites?

The world offers a lot of opportunities for billionaires and throws up few of the barriers that most of us face. In particular, world borders are porous for the billionaire set. Virtually any billionaire could, with motivation, move to nearly any country of the world—and probably acquire citizenship without much difficulty. Some scholars cast the world's elite as a "transnational capitalist class."[1] These elites are freed from the constraints of the nation-state, moving across the world through networks of global cities. The globalization of production, marketing, and finance, in this view, creates a rising mobility of the rich who see the world as an "abstract placelessness."[2] Chrystia Freeland, in her 2012 book *Plutocrats*, writes, "While capital—and capitalists—have gone global, governments . . . operate within national boundaries. Figuring out how the plutocrats are connected to the rest of us is one of the challenges of the global super-elite."[3] Have elites really "gone global" and moved beyond the reach of the nation-state? Are elites now mobile billionaires, unattached to place or nation, freely moving to whichever country offers the best combination of lifestyle and tax avoidance? Or are they embedded elites, still deeply connected to the places where they became successful?

For a look at the wealthy elite at the international level, I used the 2010 Forbes world billionaire list, which contained 1,011 of the richest people in the world at that time.[4] I followed up on each again in 2015, to see if the billionaires had moved their primary residence. The resulting data invite a series of questions. First, where in the world do billionaires live? Do they live in low-tax countries more than high-tax countries? How many billionaires have moved away from their homeland? And since 2010, how many have moved across countries? Among those that move, do they typically find their way into a low-tax country? These data give a clear view into the geographic mobility of the richest people in the world.

Where Do Billionaires Live?

If billionaires move in response to high taxes, then we would expect them to typically live in countries with low taxes. After all, most of these people have remarkable lifestyles steeped in international travel. They jet-set around the world in private planes and own multiple homes and properties across the globe. As economic elites at the top of the food chain, it should be easy for them to live wherever they want. But, most of their additional homes are unoccupied "most if not all of the time," as one expert on elite real estate put it.[5]

Despite their frequent travel, billionaires still have a primary residence. Bill Gates, for example, travels extensively, is deeply committed to philanthropy in Africa, and often attends the elite conference circuit, making appearances at Davos in Switzerland, Cannes in France, Wimbledon in London, and the TED Conference in Vancouver. Gates is reasonably described as a citizen of the world, yet he lives in Seattle—the city where he grew up and the city where he built his business. He may well own vacation properties in other countries, but his primary residence is in the United States and specifically in Washington State. In its list of the world's billionaires, Forbes identified the country of primary residence for everyone on the list except one German-born billionaire whose residency is unknown. Forbes has a team of fifty journalists in sixteen countries that "meet[s] with the list candidates and their handlers and interview[s] employees, rivals, attorneys and securities analysts."[6] The Forbes data were collected for journalistic and business-press interest, but they serve as a source of good information on the residency of the world's economic elite.

So, where do the world's billionaires live? Most frequently, they live in the United States. Some 397 of the world's billionaires—40 percent—have a primary U.S. residence. Most, but not all, of these individuals are American-born. Nine American-born billionaires live outside the country, but 37 people on the list are immigrants to America. No other country in the world comes close to matching the United States—either for billionaire residency or billionaire in-migration. In a world where tropical tax havens flourish, America remains the global center for billionaires. A full 98 percent of American-born billionaires live in the United States, and it is the leading destination for worldwide billionaires who live outside their homeland.

Moreover, the great majority of billionaires live where they were born. Out of the 1,010 world billionaires in 2010 for whom we have data, 165 live outside their country of birth (as of 2010), and 845 live in their national homeland. In other words, 84 percent of the world's billionaires live in their country of birth.

One can reasonably wonder whether this is a large or a small number. It clearly does not give much initial support to the notion that the super-rich have gone global and left behind the rules and laws of their national homelands. On the other hand, it does mean that 16 percent of billionaires migrated to a different country at some point in their lives. This is relatively high mobility compared to the general population. Globally, only 3.2 percent of the world's 7 billion people live outside their country of birth, according to data from the United Nations. In Western developed countries, about 11 percent of the population was born abroad.[7] So, billionaires are more mobile than the average person in a Western country—by about 5 percentage points.

But some occupations are far more globalized. For example, physics—the study of matter—is an academic discipline with very little content that is unique to a country. American physics professors are working on the same research problems and publishing in the same journals as French, Russian, and Chinese physics professors, and essentially all of their work is published in English. It is a truly global discipline, and among the world's top physicists, little more than half live in their country of birth (Figure 3.1).[8] A number of academic disciplines seem to have similarly high rates of international mobility, including computer science, economics, and mathematics.[9]

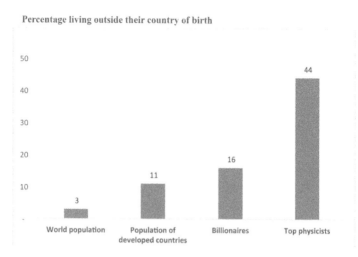

Percentage living outside their country of birth

Figure 3.1. Demographics of Global Migration, 2010. The figure compares the global migration of billionaires to that of the general world population and other key demographics. Billionaires are more mobile than the overall world population, but only a bit more mobile than the typical resident of a developed (OECD) country. In contrast, billionaires are much less mobile than top physicists—of whom almost half (44 percent) live outside their country of birth. Sources: For migration in the world and developed country populations, see United Nations (2016); for billionaires, Forbes Billionaire List (2010); for top physicists, see Hunter, Oswald, and Charlton (2009).

In comparison to physicists, billionaires are very much bound to their nations of origin. Some 16 percent of billionaires live abroad, compared to 44 percent of top physicists. The world of business and high finance is much more geographically "sticky" than is the world of science.

A Flight from Taxation?

"Billionaire retention," as one might call it, is high overall, with 84 percent of the world's billionaires "retained" in their country of birth. Do taxes on top incomes affect this retention? Do nations with high top tax rates lose more of their billionaires?

Figure 3.2 provides a simple first test of billionaire tax flight. Countries with the lowest marginal income tax rates on top earners—such as Saudi Arabia and the United Arab Emirates (UAE)—are on the left-hand side of the figure. Those with the highest tax rates—such as Denmark and Sweden—

are on the right-hand side. The size of a country's circle reflects how many billionaires were born in that country. The vertical axis shows the percentage of billionaires still living in their home country.

There is plenty of variation in billionaire retention. Hong Kong, for example, remains home to 100 percent of the billionaires who were born in the country. But Singapore is home to only 40 percent of Singapore-born billionaires. The United Kingdom (Britain) is home to over 80 percent of the billionaires born in that country, while only about 40 percent of Greek-born

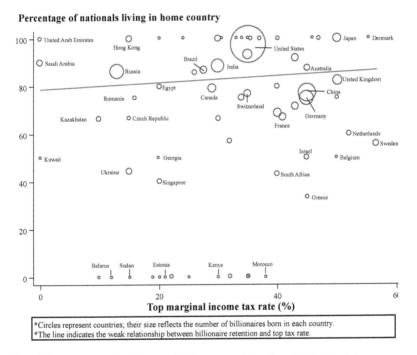

Percentage of nationals living in home country

*Circles represent countries; their size reflects the number of billionaires born in each country.
*The line indicates the weak relationship between billionaire retention and top tax rate.

Figure 3.2. **Retention of Billionaires by Country and Tax Rate, 2010.** Countries are weighted by the number of billionaires born in each country as indicated by circle size. Countries with the lowest marginal income tax rates on top earners—such as Saudi Arabia and the United Arab Emirates—are on the left-hand side. Those with the highest tax rates—such as Denmark and Sweden—are on the right. The line shows the slope of the regression of billionaire retention (%) by the top marginal income tax rate in the country. Although there is great variation in billionaire retention, top tax rates appear to be irrelevant to whether billionaires reside in their home country. Sources: Forbes Billionaire List (2010) and KPMG individual income tax rates table.

billionaires live in Greece. However, taxes seem largely irrelevant to billionaire retention. Greece and Britain have roughly the same top tax rate (over 40 percent), as do Hong Kong and Singapore (15 to 20 percent). Billionaire retention does not decline as the tax rate rises—as the mobile billionaire hypothesis predicts. If anything, there is a very slight tendency for billionaires to be more likely to remain in their home country when the tax rate is high. But the correlation is essentially zero: Top tax rates have no obvious impact on the likelihood of billionaires residing in their home country.

A second approach is to look specifically at the billionaires who have moved—those who live outside the country in which they were born. Among those who move, do taxes influence where they go? In other words, when billionaires move, do they move to places with lower taxes?

There are some easy signals that low taxation is an item of interest for the 16 percent of billionaires who have moved. A few small countries attract a disproportionate number of billionaires. Monaco, for example, is a tiny city-state with a total population of fewer than 40,000 people. Monaco does not tax residents' foreign-sourced income, making it a legendary tax haven in Europe. Four of the world's billionaires reside in Monaco—1 for every 10,000 people in the country. (By comparison, the United States has 1 billionaire for every 800,000 people.) Likewise, the tropical tax haven countries of Bermuda, the Cayman Islands, and the Bahamas each have one billionaire in residence—none born on these islands.

Two leading billionaire destinations are Britain (specifically London) and Switzerland; after the United States, they are the top destinations for billionaire migration. And both of these countries have different tax rules for high-income people born abroad. Britain has a high top income tax rate of 50 percent. However, for a small group of "non-domicile" residents, global earnings are exempt from British taxes, meaning they pay U.K. tax only on their U.K.-derived income. People who can credibly declare that their "true home" is a foreign country are exempt from taxation on their overseas income. This loophole is available only to the richest residents—it costs £90,000 (about $120,000 in U.S. dollars) to claim "non-dom" status.[10] The loophole largely allows foreign-born billionaires to bypass Britain's top tax rate. Of the world's billionaires, 23 were born in Britain, but 42 billionaires lived there in 2010—a net in-migration of 19. (This includes 4 British billionaires who live abroad and 23 foreign-born billionaires who moved to Britain.)

Switzerland has a similar loophole. Tax rates are notoriously complicated in Switzerland, but in Geneva and Zurich the top tax rate is about 34 percent. This is lower than the U.S. rate, but Switzerland is not a tax haven for the Swiss.[11] However, wealthy foreigners can negotiate a "lump sum tax" that avoids declaring their foreign assets and income. Under this arrangement, rich foreigners can declare an income equal to five times their annual housing costs. This means that someone who earns $20 million a year from international investments could well negotiate a taxable income of about $4 million and only pay income tax on that amount.[12] So, rather than paying tax on their worldwide capital incomes—as the Swiss must pay—foreigners negotiate a consumption tax based on how expensive their Swiss home is. This arrangement is controversial in Switzerland, but the tax loophole survived a 2014 referendum to repeal it.[13]

A strong majority of billionaires living in Switzerland were born abroad: 8 billionaires were born there, but 27 lived there in 2010. Of course, the fact that the people of Switzerland speak three major European languages (German, French, and Italian) also makes it an attractive and cosmopolitan destination. A large portion of Swiss billionaire in-migrants are Germans who live in its German-speaking regions. Nevertheless, Switzerland provides perhaps the most compelling evidence of billionaire tax migration.

Overall, among the 165 billionaires who live outside their country of birth, how many of them live in a country with lower taxes than the country in which they were born? Taking into account the British and Swiss tax loopholes for foreigners, some 65 percent of billionaires moved to lower-tax states. Only 35 percent moved to states with the same or higher tax rate. This 30-percentage-point gap gives a basic estimate of how much billionaire migration is driven by tax avoidance. On balance, 30 percent of billionaire migrations conferred a tax advantage.

Britain—which, for these purposes, means the city of London—and Switzerland account for 27 percent of all billionaires living outside their country of birth. These two locations—which provide tax loopholes for foreign-born billionaires—represent nearly all of the observed tax-advantageous moves. London and Switzerland combine tax avoidance with a cosmopolitan lifestyle in the most elite spaces in Europe. There are some good reasons why Europeans, in particular, have begun to feel that a global elite is exploiting tax loopholes and driving up the cost of living in the most appealing parts of the continent. However, this represents only 50 of the 1,010 individuals on the world billionaire list, or just under 5 percent.

Moreover, taxes are not the most striking feature of billionaire migration. A stronger pattern shows a process we might call "billionaire concentration." Billionaires were born in 74 different countries. However, by 2010, billionaires resided in only 57 different countries (17 fewer). Many countries in eastern Europe and Africa have global billionaires who hail

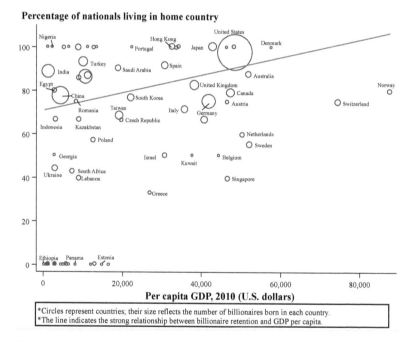

*Circles represent countries; their size reflects the number of billionaires born in each country.
*The line indicates the strong relationship between billionaire retention and GDP per capita.

Figure 3.3. Retention of Billionaires by Country and Per Capita GDP, 2010. Countries are weighted by the number of billionaires born in each country as indicated by circle size. The line shows the slope of the regression of billionaire retention (%) by per capita GDP in the country. In contrast to Figure 3.1, this figure shows that billionaire retention is strongly influenced by income levels. Sources: Forbes Billionaire List (2010), World Bank World Development Indicators Database, UN Country Profiles, and Knoema World Data Atlas.

from one of these countries but none who live there today (Kenya, Sudan, Estonia, and more).

Billionaires are also geographically concentrated in wealthier Western countries, compared to their places of birth. Billionaire retention is consistently higher among richer countries. Figure 3.3 shows billionaire retention in each country by level of per capita GDP. This graph is directly comparable to Figure 3.2 and shows that in contrast to tax rates, income levels have clear explanatory power.

When billionaires move, they have a strong tendency to move to a richer country. Over 80 percent of billionaires moved to a richer country—with a higher per capita GDP—than where they were born. Billionaires, it seems, want to be where the action is—and where the markets are.

Typologies of Billionaire Migration

It is worthwhile to pause at this point and ask a key question: Is living outside one's country of birth a sign of being a global citizen beyond the reach of the nation-state? It is tempting to think so—and for some billionaires living abroad it does reflect a strategic detachment from the policies of their home country. But in reality, many billionaires moved as children; it was their parents who made the decision to move and bore the costs of migration. Others moved for college or at the outset of their careers but never moved again. Indeed, most billionaires moved well before they attained economic success, and they live where they started their careers. For these individuals, the motivation behind moving was not avoiding taxes but rather moving with their families, moving for education, or moving to launch a career.

By examining the life stage in which billionaires moved, we can better understand how mobile they are. To study this, my research assistants and I focused on the 165 billionaires who live abroad and scoured both Forbes and the larger public records to discern when in their lives these individuals moved. There are some people for whom the approximate time of migration could not be determined. But this information is in the public records for 142 out of 165 billionaires who live abroad—or 85 percent. From this group, we can get a good sense of when in the life cycle elites typically migrate. From these data there are three basic typologies of billionaire migrants.

About 30 percent of billionaires living abroad (42 individuals) moved as children with their families. For example, Sergey Brin—the cofounder of Google—was born in Moscow and moved to the United States with his family when he was 5 years old. New York hedge fund manager Marc Lasry was born in Morocco and immigrated with his family when he was 7. Peter Thiel, cofounder of PayPal and an early Facebook investor, was born in Germany and moved to Silicon Valley with his family when he was an infant. None of these people are mobile billionaires. They were born abroad, but it was their parents who migrated; they simply live where they grew up.

A bit more than a third of billionaires abroad (55 individuals, or 39 percent) moved as adults but well before they became successful. Many immigrant billionaires moved to the United States for college or professional education and stayed in the country. Vinod Khosla—venture capitalist and cofounder of Sun Microsystems—was born in India but moved to America for professional school. Today, Khosla lives within 20 miles of Stanford University, where he received his MBA in 1982. Similarly, hedge fund manager Thomas Sandell came to the United States from Sweden for the MBA program at Columbia University, and he lives where he was trained. Media mogul Mort Zuckerman was raised in Canada; he moved to Pennsylvania for his MBA at the Wharton School and then went to law school at Harvard. After nine years as a Harvard professor, he purchased *U.S. News & World Report*. Again, these people aren't really mobile billionaires: They moved at the beginning of their careers, well before their economic success, and have stayed in the places where they became successful.

The final third of the billionaires abroad (45 individuals) moved *after* achieving strong economic success. These individuals are the mobile billionaires who use their accumulated wealth to move abroad for tax or lifestyle reasons. Richard Branson, known for Virgin Records and Virgin Atlantic, moved from Britain to the British Virgin Islands. Len Blavatnik was born in Russia, achieved early success in U.S. industry, invested heavily in Russia after the fall of communism, and ultimately moved to London with a net worth of $15 billion. These individuals are indeed mobile billionaires: They amassed great fortunes and then traversed the world in search of a cosmopolitan lifestyle and tax avoidance. Only one-third of the billionaires abroad fit this profile.

The mobile billionaires, in the end, represent little more than 5 percent of the world's richest people—about 54 individuals[14] out of more than 1,000. The mobile billionaire phenomenon occurs, but only at the margins. Public perceptions about billionaire mobility are largely mistaken, because we have let the power of the anecdote overpower the reality on the ground.

The other 95 percent of billionaires live in the country where they were born or where they launched their careers, much like everyone else. These people—the 95 percent of world billionaires who live where they became successful—are not any further beyond the reach of the nation-state than anyone else.[15]

Fast-Forward: Five-Year Migration of Billionaires

Most billionaire mobility happens early in life, well before the billionaires would be exposed to the top-tax rates in any country. Our key question is how many people move *after* achieving success, rather than moving as a child or for education. Our final test follows this question to the limit: How many people move *after* making it on the 2010 billionaire list? Have we missed key moments of mobility by looking at billionaires' past, rather than toward their future?

To test this, I tracked each billionaire from 2010 to 2015. Some of them dropped below $1 billion and were no longer on the official list, but Forbes continues to keep track of them. Similarly, some new people became billionaires during this time period, but for this analysis, I just follow the 2010 billionaire set as my sampling frame. This allows me to calculate a five-year migration rate; anyone who moves after being on the 2010 list is by definition a mobile billionaire.

Between 2010 and 2015, 18 of the 1,010 billionaires moved their primary residence to a different country—less than 2 percent migration over five years. This reaffirms that, on the whole, billionaires are not going anywhere. It also reaffirms that among the small set of mobile billionaires, tax avoidance is a common goal. More than half of these moves (10) were into tax havens such as London, Monaco, Switzerland, Singapore, and Dubai (UAE). For example, British hedge fund manager Alan Howard moved from London to Switzerland—a reminder that London is a tax haven only for the foreign "non-doms," not for British citizens. Interestingly, three moves were return migrations back from tax havens. For example, Ingvar Kamprad—founder of the Swedish furniture company Ikea—moved back to Sweden in 2014 after four decades of living in Switzerland. American hedge fund manager Louis Bacon returned to New York after a stint of London residency. And a Russian oligarch, Mikhail Gutseriev, returned home after several years of political exile in London. The remaining moves seem largely about lifestyle. For example, Australian casino billionaire James Packer moved to Los Angeles shortly before his engagement to American singer Mariah Carey.[16]

The running total of mobile billionaires adds up to 66 individuals—or 6.5 percent of the initial group.[17] Remarkably few billionaires use their wealth to relocate to a different country. Indeed, the mobile billionaire set is outnumbered by the billionaire mortality rate. By 2015, 7 percent of the 2010 billionaire list had died—more than three times the number that moved. Global billionaires are more likely to die than to move to a different country.

The evocative notion of a transnational capitalist class was largely based on anecdote and impression. Follow-up research in the transnational class literature increasingly emphasizes the continuing importance of national ties among business elites and nation-based business communities.[18] And in looking at the location and migration of billionaires, we likewise see only thin shreds of evidence for a truly transnational elite that has moved beyond the reach of the nation-state. Despite the rise of globalization and despite some clear examples of billionaire tax migration, it is still true that the rich—for the most part—live where they were born. The British elite live in Britain, the Chinese elite live in China, and the American elite live in America.

Do the Rich Move Their Money? The Role of International Tax Havens

Based on the Forbes list of the world's billionaires, the richest people in the world rarely move their primary residency to low-tax countries. But, perhaps the rich in the Western world do not need to move, because they can simply move their assets offshore. To what extent do foreign bank accounts in international tax havens provide a workable substitute for the rich—not just billionaires but top income earners more generally—to avoid taxes? Rather than moving themselves and their families, can they achieve the same tax savings by simply moving their money? If so, understanding the movement of money is at least as important as the movement of the rich themselves.

It should be noted that there is a parallel world of offshore finance used by major corporations to legally avoid corporate taxes in many countries. This is an extremely complex world of corporate accounting, involving "inversions" to obtain a foreign legal address and "transfer pricing" within a corporate structure to declare overseas profits in tax haven locations. These offshore bookkeeping games have made it more difficult to collect corporate taxes on the overseas profits of some companies—especially technology firms such as Apple and Google. However, these are quite different practices than those used by individuals for tax avoidance and evasion. Corporations operate under a different set of international rules than do individuals and have more—and more legal—ways of bypassing the national systems of corporate taxation. This chapter is about the offshore systems available to rich individuals and the challenges facing the individual income tax system.

The UBS Swiss Bank Scandal

In 2007, Bradley Birkenfeld, an American who had worked as a private banker and wealth manager for the Swiss bank UBS, came in for a meeting with prosecutors at the U.S. Department of Justice. He disclosed massive tax evasion schemes developed by the bank and how the bank marketed them to U.S. millionaires.

Based in Switzerland, Birkenfeld traveled regularly to the United States to cultivate clients. UBS sponsored art shows and yacht races as a way to meet wealthy potential clients to try to sell them tax avoidance strategies. One such client, routinely listed among the Forbes 400 richest Americans, transferred $200 million in assets to UBS, so that the investment income earned from that money could be concealed from U.S. tax authorities. UBS provided U.S. clients with credit cards to access their hidden money, and they advised that any cash withdrawals be reported as loans from UBS—not income. In one case, Birkenfeld converted his client's money into diamonds and personally carried them across the Atlantic in a tube of toothpaste.[19]

Birkenfeld was marketing Swiss bank accounts for which U.S. millionaires could follow the exact same investment strategies they were already using at home, but without reporting the earnings from their investments to the Internal Revenue Service. In 2005, UBS circulated an internal memo from its legal department, generically explaining that most aspects of Birkenfeld's job description were illegal under both U.S. law and agreements that UBS had specifically signed with the IRS. To Birkenfeld, the memo was a sign that UBS was planning to blame its employees if its business practices were discovered. He left the firm and eventually decided to disclose UBS practices under a whistleblower protection law.

The fallout was enormous. The company acknowledged its role in marketing tax evasion to rich Americans and settled for $780 million in fines. Birkenfeld's biggest client, a Russian-born American billionaire named Igor Olenicoff, was convicted of tax evasion and received a $52 million fine and two years of probation. UBS agreed to release records from 4,500 American-owned accounts, breaking a centuries-long tradition of bank secrecy. The IRS launched a voluntary disclosure program—under which 39,000 Americans have disclosed offshore accounts rather than risk prosecution—and this has yielded $5.5 billion in back taxes.[20]

Tax Evasion and Regulation

The United States and the OECD (Organisation for Economic Cooperation and Development) have been cracking down on tax havens in recent years. The UBS scandal was a key impetus—as was the Great Recession that put tremendous strain on national finances. In 2010, the United States passed the Foreign Account Tax Compliance Act, known as FATCA. This is perhaps the most serious piece of new legislation that most people have not heard of. It requires banks worldwide to report U.S. citizens' accounts or face a 30 percent withholding tax on any income the bank receives from U.S. sources. This may sound like aspirational law, but more than 100 countries—including Switzerland—have signed agreements with the United States to establish regular bank account reporting. The OECD—the club of developed countries of the world—has moved to establish the FATCA criteria as the new global standard for financial reporting. As early as 2009, the OECD commission declared the "end of bank secrecy."[21]

Yet, bank secrecy has survived. Shell companies—firms that exist only on paper and provide secret conduits between real people and foreign transactions—can still conceal who owns offshore bank accounts. The Panama

Papers, released in 2016, show that the offshore economy is alive and well. The Panama Papers involved a leak of more than 11 million files from one of the world's largest offshore law firms, Mossack Fonseca. The documents profile the secret financial lives of celebrities, top politicians, and business elites from around the world.

The Panama Papers vividly show how tax evasion occurs, and the documents are fascinating for their sophistication—shell companies inside shell companies—as well as the details of exotic locations and high-profile players. The Mossack Fonseca files show—more than anything—that there will be no armistice in millionaires' efforts to minimize their tax obligations.

In the wake of the Panama Papers, some critics insist that taxing the rich is a fruitless endeavor. "Money goes wherever it wants and guess what? It wants to go where there is no tax," said a professor of tax law at McGill University. Trying to stop tax havens is like "tilting at windmills," she says, adding "we know we can't succeed."[22] In this view, the only way to fight tax havens is to cut tax rates on the rich, in the hopes of retaining at least some of their money onshore. This is a simple variant of the mobile millionaire hypothesis: If you tax them, they will hide their money offshore.

The Offshore Economy

How accurate is this view of millionaires' money? The first thing to ask is who can use the offshore economy to their advantage. Many high income earners were asking Mossack Fonseca this question. As one individual wrote in a leaked e-mail,

> How does a US citizen legally get funds to Panama without the knowledge of the US government and how can those funds be profitably invested without the US government knowing about them?[23]

The two-pronged nature of the question is critical to understanding tax havens. Moving money from the United States into a secret offshore account does not, in itself, avoid any taxes. In the United States, most sources of income are subject to direct reporting to the IRS. Audits of tax returns show that 96 percent of income from wages, salaries, interest, and dividends are reported accurately on tax returns.[24] This is in large part because employers, businesses, and banks file direct reports to the IRS, which are used to check what people claim on their tax returns. This makes it hard to avoid taxes on income earned in America.

The tax system works on a principle that political scientist Margaret Levi calls "quasi-voluntary compliance." Taxation, as she observes, "is voluntary because taxpayers choose to pay. It is *quasi*-voluntary because the noncompliant are subject to coercion—if they are caught."[25] People are honest with the IRS when their incomes are independently reported to the tax authority—this includes virtually all wage earners, who have almost no real opportunities to evade taxation. When it comes to income sources that are not directly reported, people are more flexible with their tax returns. This includes restaurant workers who earn tips and investors who set up offshore shell companies.

There is little point in simply parking money overseas. People moving money offshore already had to pay tax on that money when they first earned it. Offshore accounts provide a platform to make investments, which generate future offshore income streams that are invisible to tax authorities. Offshored money is almost always directly invested in stocks, bonds, and mutual funds, just as if the money were in an onshore account.

As opposed to investing from an onshore account, offshoring allows one to bypass the automatic reporting of investment income to the IRS. Central to this is something called the "portfolio interest exemption."[26] Under this policy, passed in 1984, foreign persons living abroad do not owe tax on interest and dividend payments from U.S. companies. The main objective of offshore tax evasion is to make American investors look like they are foreigners to the U.S. government. As the IRS has described it, the goal is to "create structures making it appear that a nonresident alien or foreign entity is the owner of assets and income, when in fact and substance, true ownership remains with a U.S. taxpayer."[27] Using a foreign account to purchase stock allows Americans to pretend they are Europeans. This does not relieve Americans of their legal obligation to pay tax on investment income. But their interest and dividend income is not automatically reported to the IRS, giving a layer of secrecy that can be used to evade the income tax.

The portfolio interest exemption is essentially a loophole in the tax code that creates business for international lawyers, investment advisors, and accountants. It is part of what political scientist Jeffrey Winters calls the Income Defense Industry. This industry deploys "legions of professionals and lobbyists to insert material into the tax code that is favorable" to top income earners.[28] They then sell legal and accounting "products" designed to exploit these loopholes in the tax system to those who can afford them.

In recent years, a corollary political campaign has cut the budget of the IRS, undermining auditing resources and making a host of complex tax evasion schemes—including offshoring—a safer bet for high income earners. A collection of well-funded super-PACs and some leading conservative politicians advocate for the complete elimination of the IRS, calling it a "rogue agency."[29] Between 2010 and 2016, the IRS saw funding cuts of $1.2 billion, forcing a layoff of one-quarter of its auditing staff. A recent letter coauthored by seven former IRS commissioners—including commissioners under presidents Ronald Reagan, George H.W. Bush, and George W. Bush—raised alarms over the scale of the cuts. "Over the last fifty years," the commissioners wrote, "none of us has ever witnessed anything like what has happened to the IRS [budget] . . . over the last five years."[30] The result is an agency that is ill prepared to audit the complex tax returns and systems of shell companies of the richest Americans.

The offshore economy is specifically for "capitalists": those who make their money from owning capital, rather than from labor. Most millionaires in the United States are the working rich, and few earn large amounts of income from capital. People committing serious tax evasion with these accounts are the very richest of the rich—largely among the top 10 percent of the millionaire set. Most millionaires do not make their money through capital, and the offshore economy does not provide a pathway to significantly reduce their state or federal tax burden.

Still, the richest 10 percent of the U.S. millionaire set represents about 50,000 people. So how large is the offshore economy? Recent work by Berkeley economist Gabriel Zucman gives a rigorous view into the offshore world. Across a series of academic articles and a book titled *The Hidden Wealth of Nations*, Zucman documents the size of the global tax haven industry.

How does one study an industry whose job it is to make things invisible? When rich people hide large amounts of money overseas, it creates anomalies in international financial accounting statistics. Just as black holes distort light and gravity in ways astronomers can detect, tax havens distort international accounting statistics in ways that leave a visible trace of their existence and size.

Countries maintain detailed statistics on foreign investments. For example, corporations like Google and Intel directly report to the U.S. government how much of their stock is owned by foreign entities. The IMF aggregates this data to create international accounts of cross-border investments around the world. A flaw in this system is that when Swiss bankers purchase stock in U.S. companies, it is recorded on the Swiss side only if the so-called beneficial owner of the account is Swiss. If Swiss bankers are acting on behalf of foreign clients, the stock purchase is not reported as a Swiss asset. The *sale* of the stock is always reported by U.S. corporations, but the *purchase* is not recorded in any foreign country.

Globally, more stocks and bonds are sold than are officially purchased. Asset sales to a foreign entity are reported, but in some cases no foreign country reports the purchase. In accounting terms, there are more global liabilities than global assets. Similarly, more cross-border interest and dividend payments are made than are officially received. These accounting errors are the trace of international tax havens. They are the sign of money disappearing into the offshore world.

Zucman uses these imbalances to estimate the amount of wealth hidden in offshore havens. The imbalances—summed across the world's financial statistics—amount to $7.6 trillion. This is a staggering number. By comparison, however, the global stock of financial wealth is about $95 trillion. So, about 8 percent of global financial wealth is hidden in the offshore economy.[31]

Is the Term "Tax Haven" a Misnomer?

Gabriel Zucman has argued that the offshore economy is fundamentally about tax evasion. However, some of his evidence gives important signs to the contrary. Tax havens help people avoid taxes, but that's not the only thing they do, and maybe that's not even the most important thing they do. Consider the analogy of movie theaters and popcorn. Popcorn is a big thing at movie theaters—every movie theater in America has popcorn, and almost no other place serves popcorn warm. Places that show movies could reasonably be called "popcorn theaters." This raises the question, why do people go to the movies? Is it more for the movie or more for the popcorn? The price of popcorn is similar to the price of a movie ticket, but popcorn is probably not the primary draw for most customers. So, if we called these places "popcorn theaters," that would be sort of right, but it would be missing a big part of the picture.

In the world of secret offshore finance, there is similar ambiguity over which is the primary product and which is the secondary product. In other words, is tax avoidance the movie or the popcorn?

Tax haven countries are, technically, selling only *bank secrecy* to wealthy clients, not tax evasion directly. Tax evasion is the act of *not* declaring your taxable income—it can be done only by the individual tax filer. Swiss banks and Panamanian law firms have conspired and been complicit in tax evasion, but the immediate product they are selling is secrecy. In the Panama Papers, one lawyer described a big client by saying,

> He is the manager of one of the richest hedge funds in the world. . . . [The p]rimary objective is to maintain the utmost confidentiality and ideally to open bank accounts without disclosing his name as a private person.[32]

In this sense, tax havens are better understood as "secrecy jurisdictions"— they conceal things.[33]

What do wealthy people want to do with secrecy? Tax avoidance is only one reason why the rich seek out secrecy and anonymity—and it may not be the most important reason.

Secrecy for Other Reasons

Emma Watson, the actress who played Hermione in the Harry Potter movies, used Mossack Fonseca to set up a shell company registered in the British Virgin Islands. She named the company "Falling Leaves Ltd." At some point, she transferred several million of her after-tax earnings to the company. Falling Leaves then purchased a three-bedroom, £2.8 million home in London in 2013. Now, in the publicly available Land Registry in Britain, the owner of this home is listed as "Falling Leaves Ltd." rather than as Emma Watson.[34] Falling Leaves still has to pay property taxes on the residence. This is a simple story of a well-known celebrity trying to maintain personal privacy and prevent legions of Harry Potter fans from being able to look up her address on the Internet.

Of course, a tax advantage could occur in the future. When Falling Leaves sells the residence, any likely capital gains from the sale will not be automatically reported to tax authorities. So, it is possible that Watson set up the shell company in order to evade taxes on the expected gains from the future sale of her London home. But thanks to the Panama Papers leak, Falling Leaves is no longer an anonymous shell company, and Ms. Watson will have to declare any income her "company" makes in the future. But probably more salient to Ms. Watson is that now Harry Potter fanatics can look up her address in the public Land Registry.

The appeal of anonymity goes beyond celebrities and may involve murkier motivations, like hiding money from litigation, creditors, or messy divorces.[35] Desire for secrecy is most tellingly shown by the high rate of tax haven use by residents of Middle Eastern countries that have no income tax.

Internationally, there are large differences in the offshoring of wealth across countries. The central banks of Switzerland and some other tax haven countries have issued aggregate reports of the national origin of account holders. Zucman used these reports to calculate the share of national financial wealth that residents of different countries keep in the offshore economy (Figure 3.4). Around major regions of the world, the share of financial wealth held in offshore accounts ranges from as little as 4 percent to as high as 57 percent. Zucman himself had little to say about these regional patterns, but the differences are striking.[36]

If the offshore economy is primarily about tax avoidance, then offshoring should be highest in the countries with the highest tax rates. The evidence suggests the opposite.

Residents of the Arab oil kingdoms of Saudi Arabia, Kuwait, Qatar, and the United Arab Emirates are the most intensive users of tax havens in the world. In these countries, more than half of total financial wealth is in offshore accounts (57 percent). This wealth is owned by the royal families of these kingdoms. They are absolute rulers and have decreed the tax rates they wish to pay. None of these countries has an income tax, so there is no tax advantage in maintaining shell companies and offshore accounts. The money is held offshore for some non-tax reason. Largely, it seems offshore accounts are used to act anonymously—to purchase Western companies and real estate without their identities being revealed. The purpose is to avoid un-

Percentage of national financial wealth held in offshore accounts

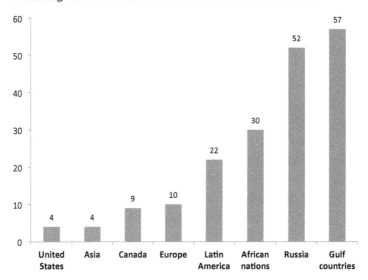

Figure 3.4. Use of Offshore Accounts. There are large differences in the offshoring of wealth across countries. This figure shows the share of national financial wealth that residents of different countries keep in the offshore economy. The evidence suggests that countries with the highest tax rates are not the ones offshoring their wealth. Source: Zucman (2015), Table 1.

wanted attention and scrutiny. For Gulf-state royal families, Switzerland and Panama are not tax havens but purely secrecy jurisdictions.

Residents of Russia are the second-most likely to use offshore accounts. Some 52 percent of Russian financial wealth is held in offshore accounts. Yet Russia has very low income taxes on the rich—a flat tax of 13 percent. This once-communist country is remarkably free of progressive tax policies and does little to curtail the rampant inequality that emerged after the collapse of the Soviet Union. Russian political figures boast about having lower tax rates than the West and have speculated that many Westerners will eventually move to Russia to reduce their tax burden. But Russia also has something that might well worry the rich: Vladimir Putin.

Offshore accounts offer some promise of asset protection against expropriation by arbitrary dictators and regime instability. Vladimir Putin, shortly after assuming power in Russia, convened a meeting with the nation's oligarchs. The oligarchs are a mostly unlikable collection of Russian businessmen who plundered billions from the country's natural resource wealth during the turbulent privatization years and transition from communism. In this early meeting, Putin told the oligarchs that they could keep their wealth as long as they stayed out of politics and out of his way. Those who failed to heed this message have paid a heavy price.[37] Mikhail Khodorkovsky, the very richest of the oligarchs, began a quiet campaign to challenge Putin's growing authoritarianism, including funding opposition parties. In 2003, Khodorkovsky was arrested on charges of fraud, his assets were frozen, and he was eventually convicted and spent nine years in prison. Nine of Khodorkovsky's top associates had a similar fate. The oligarchs do not challenge Putin anymore.[38]

Many African elites in autocratic countries also hide a large portion of their countries' financial wealth offshore (30 percent), and probably for much the same reasons as the Russians: Their regimes could turn on them and expropriate their assets, a significant part of their wealth may be derived from corrupt dealings, and a change in authority could destroy their political protection. Sheltering assets from dubious governments is closely tied with concealing ill-gotten gains. Wealthy people in Russia and many African countries often face such concerns, which likely drive the high use of offshoring. Hiding wealth in offshore accounts seems closely connected with the problem of the "resource curse": Natural resources such as oil and diamonds often seem to doom countries to autocratic regimes, poor economic development, and high inequality. In this sense, offshoring wealth seems to be a marker of the resource curse.

The third main motivation of offshoring is, of course, tax evasion. That brings us to Europe and the United States where taxes are higher, but a much lower proportion of wealth is held offshore. Probably most of the American and European wealth that is hidden in offshore accounts is there to evade taxes on investment income. But the higher-tax countries with stronger institutional governance—the United States, Canada, and western Europe—use tax havens the least: 10 percent of European financial wealth, 9 percent of Canadian wealth, and just 4 percent of U.S. wealth is held offshore.

Overall, Figure 3.4 gives the impression that the offshore economy is more about secrecy than tax evasion. Countries with light or nonexistent taxation—Russia and the Gulf oil states—use tax havens the most: Over half of their financial wealth is held offshore. The lowest use of offshoring is mostly in the West, which represents the nation-states with the highest tax rates on top incomes.[39] This runs completely in opposition to a narrative of tax evasion.

At the same time, Western countries—represented in Figure 3.4 as Europe, Canada, and the United States—have most of the world's financial wealth. For example, Canada has more financial wealth than Russia and more wealth than all of the African continent combined. Despite the comparatively low use of offshore accounts, Western wealth accounts for more than half (54 percent) of the world's offshored financial wealth. From the perspective of offshore tax planners and wealth managers, around half of their work is helping Western clients reduce taxes on their investment income.

The offshore economy represents a mix of mostly unsavory motivations, ranging from secrecy to corruption to tax evasion. Sometimes there are purely innocuous reasons for using the offshore system of secret accounts, but much of it is ethically and legally questionable.

In aggregate, the offshore economy is a small-time player. Less than 10 percent of global financial wealth is held offshore, and only about half of that is clearly motivated by tax flight. The other 95 percent of the world's financial wealth—for the most part—lives by the rules and tax policies set by national laws.

Slow Globalization

Despite some leakage from tax havens and global mobility, millionaire taxes are an effective means of raising revenue and addressing inequality. There is, to be sure, movement of people and money at the top of the global economy. This movement is in part a shift away from national policies that tax and regulate the rich. Globally, we see that about 5 or 6 percent of the world's billionaires are mobile elites, who geographically move to avoid taxes, and also that about 5 percent of the world's financial wealth readily disappears into the offshore economy for tax purposes. Globalization is giving the powerful more ways to shelter their incomes from nation-based tax policies. Yet, these ways remain limited, and the rich remain largely embedded in their national economies.

The mobile millionaire hypothesis has found a rare consensus in the U.S. political discourse. The left seeks to portray top income earners as greedy and unpatriotic capitalists gouging honest taxpayers. The right seeks to portray the tax system as a hopelessly unenforceable mess that should be swept away. Both sides converge on a shared narrative of mobile millionaires, but for different ideological reasons. There is some truth in each view. But both sides are searching for a crisis that does not really exist.

Place as a Form of Capital

4

Why is place important for the rich? The 1 percent—people who draw the very highest incomes in society—have economic freedom to move and live wherever they want. Yet, they rarely exercise this freedom. For the most part, the rich live in the places where they started out. Economic elites often maintain a busy travel schedule, but few make a permanent residence outside of their country of birth. Within the United States, the migration of millionaires is lower than among the general public, and much lower than among the poor. U.S. states with more progressive income taxes have no fewer millionaires than do states with flat taxes. In the rare occasions of elite migration, top earners do indeed pay attention to the tax rate of their destination state, but the effect of taxes on migration is small. In general, the rich are deeply attached to the places where they become successful.

Place attachment has implications that go well beyond tax policy and that help us understand the nature of mobility and elite status in a globalized world. The mobile millionaire thesis, despite its intuitive appeal, is largely wrong. Top income earners are much better understood as embedded elites: It is not that they never move but that they are strongly resistant to moving.

This chapter aims to develop an economic sociology of place that will help us understand why millionaire migration is so rare.[1] For people with economic success, place is an advantage and an economic asset—a form of intangible capital that yields economic returns. Place is part of how social boundaries form between insiders and outsiders. Place is a container for opportunities that are not readily available to outsiders. Moving often means giving up place-specific capital and a home-field advantage, while becoming an outsider somewhere else. Such moves can make economic sense for some people—such as those making below-market earnings for their work—but it rarely makes sense for those who have already achieved exceptional economic success.

One simple reason why the rich are grounded in place is because, as seen in Chapter 1, they tend to have a lot of family responsibilities: They are much more likely to be married and to have children at home. And the reality is that people with families move less often. For some readers, this might be a fully adequate explanation of low millionaire migration. And in my conversations with millionaires—who sometimes e-mail me with unsolicited feedback when my research receives press coverage—they typically agree that family responsibilities explain their limited mobility.

However, something deeper and more interesting is going on. People develop a strong home-field advantage that grows over time in the place where they live and work. As people advance in their careers, the advantage to remaining in their local area grows. The wealthy accumulate both human capital and social capital that have the highest returns in the place where they developed them. Moving away means giving up intangible resources—contacts, social currency, and insider knowledge—that are crucial to both status and economic success. Place grows as an asset over the course of one's economic life. The more money people make, the greater the risk of giving up home-field advantage by moving away.

This has important implications for how we understand the role of borders in the modern world. Much of social scientific thinking about borders focuses on the legal walls between rich and poor countries and the barriers limiting the movement of poor people into rich countries. Millionaire migration, however, is almost entirely about migration *between* rich countries—movement from higher to lower tax places within the OECD (or between different regions in rich countries). As we will see, globalization has not really mattered for these borders. Over the last thirty years, the West has seen considerable growth of immigration from the global South. However, there has been virtually no rise in migration *between* rich countries. Even grand experiments in free mobility—the creation of European citizenship and the dissolving of their internal borders—mattered little for where people chose to live.

Top income earners today have the means and freedom to live almost anywhere they wish. But like the citizens of European countries when the borders were opened, they remain where their home-field advantage lies. Between the well-off places of the world, the legal borders are not holding back meaningful migration flows. What does hold back migration among the prosperous—and what holds Western countries together in this time of globalization—is not legal borders but rather place-specific human and social capital that embeds people in the places where they invest their early lives and careers.

Why People Move

There are a thousand idiosyncratic, personal reasons why individuals move. But systematic migration pressures are mostly driven by opportunity differentials. Some places offer much greater chances of economic success than do others. Internationally, migration almost uniformly flows from countries with low incomes into countries with high incomes. Typically, this represents the global poor moving into rich nations, where migrants will earn three to four times the wages they would earn at home.[2]

In many of the world's poorest countries, such as India, few people earn as much money as the poor in the United States or western Europe. The richest 5 percent in India earn less than the poorest 5 percent in America.[3] India has some extremes of inequality—and some billionaires—but only a tiny fraction of the population approaches the living standards of the West. In the worldwide income pyramid, what matters most is not what skills people have or what kind of job they hold, but simply where they live and work. People who live and work in a rich country earn a large "location premium," whereas almost everyone in a poor country pays a large "location penalty."[4] For those born in the West—or who are able to move to the West—place is a form of intangible capital that pays remarkable dividends.

These opportunity differentials are a central motivation for cross-border movement. People want to move when they have a poor economic fit with a place, or perhaps more precisely, when they would have a better economic fit someplace else.

Sandwiches and Software

Skills and location can be hard to disentangle. People in high-income places usually have higher skills and education than do those in low-income places. And it is easy to think that people in poor countries earn low incomes because of limited human capital. This is, of course, partly true, but it is only one piece of the story. A central problem for the world's poor is that their skills are in the wrong location.

Comparing McDonald's workers around the world provides an intriguing examination of location premiums. McDonald's restaurants are highly standardized across different countries. Their workers do essentially identical jobs, create the same products, and work with the same technology, whether they are in the United States, Mexico, or China. And the local price of a Big Mac gives a standard metric of real pay.

Economist Orley Ashenfelter recognized the potential for McDonald's restaurants to show how place matters in determining real wages. He asked: How many Big Macs could a worker buy *from his or her own restaurant* for each hour the person worked? In the United States, an hour's work at McDonald's gives enough purchasing power for 2.4 Big Macs—roughly the same as in Canada and western Europe. In Russia, an hour's work at McDonald's pays half as much (1.2 Big Macs). In Asia, the Middle East, and Latin America, an hour's work will buy only one-third to one-half of a Big Mac. In real terms, a McDonald's worker in the West is paid almost seven times as much as someone doing exactly the same job in India or Latin America.[5]

These kinds of opportunity differentials are central to why people are motivated to move. Real wage differences between rich and poor countries are a tremendous pull factor in migration. For McDonald's workers around the world, their pay is not determined by their skills, human capital, effort, or initiative; instead, it is largely determined by where they perform their job. This, in turn, is mostly about for whom the sandwiches are made: Who are their customers?

Computer programmers see similar benefits to location. Programmers in India are among the small fraction of that country's population who earn higher real wages than do poor people in the United States. However, when Indian programmers migrate to America, they earn dramatically higher pay.

Overseas programmers apply for H-1B visas to work onsite in the United States. Because the number of visas is very limited, the applications effectively become lotteries. Indian programmers who win the visa lottery, and are able to work in the United States, go on to earn about $55,000 more annually than people who lose the lottery.[6] This is a roughly sixfold increase in pay. Cost-of-living differences roll back some of these gains. But the world for computer programmers is much like it is for McDonald's workers: Where they do their job makes a great difference in how well they are paid.

In a globalized world, programming is a very different task than making sandwiches, and not just because it requires higher skill. Technology links programmers with their clients in a way that should dissolve geographic distance. Sandwiches must be made at the customers' location. Software, however, can be made anywhere and instantly transferred to a client over the Internet. Yet, programmers still experience very large economic benefits to being in the same location as their clients—just like sandwich makers. They benefit from being where the action is.

Income Depends on Where You Live

In striking contrast to what we know about global migration, economic models of tax migration usually assume that people's income "belongs to them" and is unaffected by where they live. In technical terms, these models assume that income is exogenous to place.[7] In the abstract, this complex-sounding assumption is intuitively appealing. We tend to think that our "worth," or our income-earning capacity, is something internal to us: It is the sum of our education and training, our skills and experience, our work ethic and social skills. When we move, we take all of our personal attributes with us, so our income-earning capacity should travel with us as well. If earning potential is purely due to individual factors like skills and work ethic, then people's earning power is independent of where they live: A person working in Silicon Valley would earn essentially the same income doing the same job in Tampa. In this framework, moving to avoid taxes can reduce a person's tax rate but would not otherwise affect earnings. In policy debates, this idea that place is irrelevant to earning power is often taken for granted.

Debates over California's millionaire tax showcase the pitfalls in this line of reasoning. David Kline, a spokesman for the California Taxpayers Association, told the *New York Times* that "if you moved from California to Florida, and you are in a high-income bracket, you are automatically giving yourself a 13.3 percent raise."[8]

Kline's math is wrong for a number of reasons.[9] But the deepest problem is that California—like most states—taxes all income earned in California, regardless of where people live. So, to enjoy the low-tax rates of Florida, one must sever economic ties to California and find a way to earn that same income in the state of Florida. Moving to a lower tax regime is not "automatically giving yourself a raise." Top income earners can move, but they cannot necessarily take their income with them. For a Silicon Valley programmer, moving to Tampa would be a disastrous career choice, unless the plan was to retire. Technology workers moving to Florida would face large cuts in pay and career prospects.

Intangible Capital and Immobile Income

When thinking of elite migration, there is a crucial distinction between income (a flow) and wealth (a stock). The difference between income and wealth is similar to the difference between workers and retirees. Accumulated financial wealth is easily moved, but income is much harder to relocate.

When the rich speak of moving to avoid taxes on income, they are viewing income as their personal property—something they could earn anywhere in the world. But elites "own" only their past income—and even then, only the portion that was saved. A person who has accumulated $1 million in financial assets can take that money anywhere (as shown in Chapter 3, it is easy to move financial wealth offshore). But people do not own their annual income in the same sense—they have to produce it each year. People who move cannot simply take their income with them. Strictly speaking, this would be like a worker telling her boss, "I'm quitting—and I'm taking my salary with me." Future income does not yet belong to elites, and they cannot move it around the world as if it were their personal property.

The idea that income is independent of place is a critical flaw in the thinking about tax migration of economic elites. Today, most elite income earners are the working rich. They do not live off their accumulated or inherited wealth, but live on earnings from employment. They work as managers, financial executives, accountants, lawyers, and doctors. A popular saying among Wall Street traders is "we eat what we kill"—an excessive metaphor for saying "we are paid on commission." This makes the point well enough that income is not owned: It depends on being a top athlete in the best hunting grounds. People often fail to appreciate the advantages they have in the place where they live and how difficult it can be to walk away from success and rebuild an economic life in a new place.

Social scientists identify two central types of "intangible capital"—advantages that help facilitate career success: human capital and social capital. Human capital is largely contained within an individual, reflecting the person's skills, knowledge, training, and work ethic. Social capital extends beyond the individual to include personal connections to others that facilitate access to jobs, information, trust, and opportunities. Both are important in the creation of elite income, and both can be embedded in place—meaning that they can have value in one place but not in another.

Some types of work require high levels of professional skill, dense networks of interpersonal relations, and strong cultural fluency. These resources can be critical for job access, on-the-job productivity, or both, particularly in elite client-facing jobs or those that involve complex and collaborative problem solving. The greater the amount of social and human capital required for a job, the more place-specific components are likely to matter for ongoing success and opportunity. This, in turn, means that elite jobs are often not available to people who were trained elsewhere, who are locally unknown, whose social connections are located somewhere else, and who have better cultural fit elsewhere.

This is why so few of the world's billionaires move abroad after achieving success at home: A move could mean diluting their social and professional capital and displacing their local market skills and knowledge. Achieving extraordinary success in one place does not make one a global superstar who can work the same magic anywhere in the world. On the contrary, elites are typically talented individuals who have an extraordinary fit with their current work in their current place. Moving away may well break that fit. For people who are already highly successful, retaining their home-field advantage seems more valuable than exercising their freedom to live abroad.

The Division of Labor

Of the multiple reasons why income can depend on place, the common foundation for all is the division of labor in society. In the modern world, all work is collaborative in nature. Virtually no goods or services are produced entirely by a single individual. Almost everyone's work depends on the contributions of others. Income is not a purely individual accomplishment.

For example, construction workers build houses, but a well-built house is a joint product that depends on the effort and diligence of many co-workers. Similarly, doctors work to improve their patients' health, but they do so as one component within an overall health-care system that requires the expertise of other specialists (such as nurses, radiologists, anesthesiologists, and many more). Professors work to educate college students, but each professor typically offers only one or two of the more than thirty courses students take in their college years. Throughout the economy, individual workers make incremental contributions to something larger.

Often, we are so focused on doing our own jobs that we fail to appreciate how much our work is a joint product. We tend to internalize success and often fail to acknowledge the tremendous value in having great collaborators and coworkers.

Income depends on place because productivity depends on coworkers. Getting the job done involves other people. As a result, choosing where to live is not just a matter of personal preference but involves coordinating our lives with others. As John Donne said, "No man is an island."

Because of the importance of social capital and team production in the creation of elite income, top-level earning power is not anyone's personal property; it cannot be taken wherever the person wishes to move.

Place-Based Human Capital

The value of human capital—education, skills, and training—is not constant across places. Even if we think of people purely as a skill set in a world market for labor and talent, their skills have different productivity and value in different places.

At first glance, this idea defies conventional wisdom. Human capital is privately owned and travels without limitation. People take their human capital with them anywhere they move. However, human capital is often most valued in the place where it was acquired.

Educational institutions tend to prepare young people for the kinds of jobs available in their local region (in part by developing partnerships with local employers), and people typically seek out training and credentials that are valued where they live. Moreover, human capital tends to become more place-specific over time, as people gain experience and expertise in their occupations and with their local employers. This provides a key reason for why migration is a young person's game: Migration becomes less attractive with age, as people's skills become increasingly place-specific and more useful in their home region compared to abroad. Places become sticky over time.

Lawyers, for example, who pass the bar exam in California cannot practice law in other states—much less in other countries. The bar exam certifies their knowledge of local laws, not the laws of other places. Legal training is a combination of general skills that are transferable to other places and place-specific knowledge that is of limited value abroad. Admission to the bar in California is a home-field advantage that makes moving to other states less attractive.

This issue is much broader than just the field of legal practice. Some form of occupational licensing applies to 29 percent of the U.S. workforce.[10] Moreover, most occupational certifications are set at the state level, creating problems of credential portability. Many occupations require a person to re-certify and learn different standards after moving across states. Internationally, many people are unable to practice their profession after migrating and have to retake their entire professional training. People trained as physicians in many developing countries cannot practice medicine in the West. This is partly sensible, as the standards of medicine are very different in India or China than in the United States. But it is also partly a waste of human capital, as overseas medical training provides some general skills and knowledge that are portable and useful in other places.

In many fields, the degree of place-specific knowledge is such that one might be a master practitioner in one's home country but a lower-level apprentice abroad. This is not just true for those with high-level skills. Between rich and poor countries, some similar-sounding jobs are often performed very differently. For example, the practice of automotive repair is notably different in Guatemala and the United States. U.S. mechanics spend little time rebuilding carburetors but a great deal of time working with complex computer diagnostic equipment. So, auto mechanics have a combination of general skills that they take with them as they move and place-specific skills that are valued mostly in their home region.

Business acumen might be seen as a highly portable form of human capital: Sound business judgment and management skills are valuable everywhere. Yet, business success also depends on insight into local market opportunities; intuition about the appeal of different products and services in a location; and knowledge of a region's commercial laws, regulations, customs, and practices. So, successful people in business have some combination of general business knowledge and skills, as well as local specialization in the types of business transactions that happen in particular places and particular markets. At least some portion of business knowledge—possibly a large portion—is specific to a local market or industry and has the highest payoff in that region.

There are wide "varieties of capitalism" around the world.[11] Capitalism is a different game in the United States, Europe, and Asia. All these regions are running different forms of capitalism, under different institutional rules and practices. The kinds of knowledge, abilities, and instincts that make American business elites successful at home are different from the set of competencies needed to excel in Europe or China or Brazil. So it is for American lawyers, accountants, and real estate developers. These professions operate very differently in other countries. A top-ranked American lawyer would be of limited value in an English courtroom and would be readily defeated by a middling English barrister. American real estate developers in Italy would be paralyzed by the Italian legal commitment to preserving heritage and would be at a loss to navigate the system.

Even within the United States, there are smaller but still distinguishable varieties of capitalism between New York, Texas, and California. There is regional agglomeration of industries that make business operate differently in different parts of the country. This does not mean that migration can never work or that people lose all of their business acumen when they move across states or overseas. But regional specialization of business practices and local-market knowledge is a home-field advantage that is given up when one moves away.

In general, people who launch their careers in a place tend to have high economic fit for their skills and knowledge—a fit that only deepens over time. Human capital is partly place-specific, and it doesn't travel well when the rules of the game are different elsewhere. However, perhaps the largest home-field advantage the rich accumulate is their social capital.

Social Capital

Economic opportunities are embedded in social ties.[12] For many people, one's social network—ranging from strong family connections to loose ties with acquaintances—plays a key role in access to jobs, trust, and opportunities. Income-earning capacity derives not just from individual talent and human capital but also from *place-based social capital*—social and business connections to colleagues, collaborators, clients, funders, and cofounders. Finding a job, developing an idea, learning about market opportunities, and building a business are activities that happen through social networks.

Social capital is embodied in personal connections, reputation, goodwill, and the ability to solicit cooperation and reciprocity. Social capital allows people to share information, manage conflicts, and build alliances—it builds bridges between individuals and creates access to opportunities. The process of becoming a powerful insider is one of investing in social capital, becoming known, creating trust, and building reputation. Social capital can serve to increase productivity and solve market failures, allowing new economic activity that would not occur in the absence of interpersonal trust. Social capital can also be a form of opportunity hoarding that prevents competition from outsiders and increases inequality. Either way, social capital is valuable to those who have it. People's social capital is inevitably higher where they live and are known and lower in the other places they could move to. Moreover, advanced-career individuals tend to have accumulated vastly more social capital than people at the beginning of their careers.

A distinctive feature of social capital is that it is not subject to personal ownership—it is a resource, but not a form of property. Social capital is not owned by anyone. Moreover, social capital does not easily travel with individuals and partly depends on co-location with others.

Entrepreneurs, for example, tend to cluster and thrive in their "home" markets where they have deep roots and social ties.[13] Some of this may well reflect the value of local-market knowledge (place-specific human capital). However, cofounders and other allies are often critical to a successful entrepreneurial enterprise,[14] and successful teamwork is difficult to accomplish without face-to-face interaction and co-presence. Despite modern communications technology, distance is still an impediment to communication, collaboration, information sharing, and trust.[15]

When economic success is a joint product—rather than a purely individual accomplishment—potential migrants face a difficult network coordination problem: One's own willingness to migrate must align with that of cofounders, collaborators, and clients. Migrating away from these social connections is costly. Similarly, if one is looking for a job or business opportunities in New York, social connections in Ohio or North Carolina are of little value. Social contacts in New York are what is needed; contacts in other places are a very poor substitute for local connectedness. As sociologists Michael Dahl and Olav Sorenson document, social capital depreciates as it moves away from the places and regions where it was developed.[16]

A similar problem of elite professionals moving across firms has been documented in depth by Harvard business professor Boris Groysberg in his book *Chasing Stars*. When top-ranked Wall Street analysts change firms—moving, say, from Goldman Sachs to Merrill Lynch—there is often a sharp drop in their performance.[17] These elite analysts are typically lured away with enormous salary increases, but they struggle to find their footing within the new company, and many never return to their peak performance. Top analysts have large supporting teams behind them, and learning to work with a new team after becoming a star is often difficult: "It's a bit like a baseball pitcher traded away from the Yankees," as one business insider commented. "These people often are totally unaware of the enormous support system they had going for them . . . and are . . . initially lost and bewildered without it."[18] Talent, Groysberg concludes, is a joint product rather than an individual attribute. Investment banks do better when they cultivate stars from within the firm, rather than trying to purchase star analysts from other companies. Peak performance often does not travel with the individual.

Social capital has similar consequences as place-specific human capital, but it happens through a broader mechanism: Migration means moving away from places where one is relatively embedded to places where one is unknown and disconnected. This might be welcomed as a fresh start in some cases, such as for people looking for a second chance after some past mistakes. Ex-prisoners, for example, seem to especially benefit from migration after leaving prison, rather than returning to the same social networks and environment that lead to their incarceration.[19] But for people who have been highly successful in a field or region, migration means giving up home-field advantage—local social capital—and risking downward social mobility.

Individuals who achieve top incomes, in this view, are deeply embedded insiders who yield remarkable returns in part because of their social placement in a localized economic world. On the surface, it seems counterintuitive that success diminishes mobility, but it does reduce the likelihood of moving. Earning top-level income makes individuals more tied, rather than less tied, to the place where they built their careers. Often, the most successful are in a socioeconomic niche that works uncommonly well.

Cultural Fit

One element of social capital is culture. Sometimes culture is treated as distinct enough from social capital to deserve a separate analysis. But for the purposes of understanding millionaire migration, we regard cultural fit as an element of social capital. Cultural fit—mastery of the local ways of comfortable interaction—shapes one's ability to build new social ties and networks in an unknown place. Migration often means moving from a place where one has a high level of cultural fit to a place where the culture is less familiar. This can produce consequences ranging from a subtle sense of social differences to a deep sense of isolation and exclusion. It may lead to slight misunderstandings and miscommunications or to incapacitating language and communication barriers.

Cultural fit affects a person's access to good jobs and other opportunities, and its absence is an economic barrier to mobility. For example, top investment banks, law firms, and management consulting companies hire their high-skill workers in significant part based on cultural fit.[20] With many high-skill individuals applying for openings, firms like Goldman Sachs and Deloitte openly invoke hiring criteria such as which candidate they would most like to have a beer with or who would be best to be stuck in an airport with.

Work teams with greater cultural fit may well have higher productivity and work better together.[21] But, this comes at the cost of excluding "outsider" talent and skills. It is often unclear how much cultural fit is needed to sustain productivity in collaborative work systems and how much a focus on cultural fit is simply a way of excluding outsiders from a privileged socioeconomic circle. But for the outsider, the reasons are immaterial.

There are small-to-moderate cultural differences within most countries and often large differences across countries. Cultural differences between New York and Connecticut are barely perceptible. But between New York and Kentucky, a cultural difference—and tension—is palpable. People who grew up in Kentucky would find it difficult to work their way into an elite job in New York without being culturally pre-processed by an East Coast private boarding school[22] and/or an Ivy League university.[23] Obviously, the greatest differences are across countries; such cultural differences—starting with language—can be extremely difficult to overcome, making economic opportunities mostly inaccessible.

Even with a shared language, accents can produce subtle barriers. Americans overseas in other English-speaking countries readily distinguish themselves by their accent, which can quickly evoke stereotypes. As one American living in England commented, "As soon as you open your mouth in London, the accent comes out . . . and the recognition comes up from the person across the room. 'Oh, I'm dealing with an American.'"[24] An American with dual citizenship living in England elaborated on the accent problem:

> Now, I kind of want a British accent. . . . I want it for a very specific reason. . . . I was trying to become a magistrate here and which is like a judge, basic level judge and . . . anyone can do it here if you're an English citizen and you're willing to volunteer. . . . However, I was at the interview and the guy . . . stared at me like are you kidding me? Because they're not going to let someone who sounds like me . . . very American . . . be the gateway to their legal system . . . be the face of their legal system. . . . [T]he guy was just staring at me at the interview, like never, never in a million years am I saying yes to this.[25]

The intangible, nonlegal barriers to living abroad come through vividly in Adrian Favell's interviews with young European mobiles. Favell describes these mobiles as "Eurostars" living in "Eurocities"—the most adventurous young Europeans moving abroad to the most cosmopolitan European places. Their lived experience is often difficult. One young woman, a German professional working in Amsterdam, spoke of feeling alienated after years in the city:

> She is finding it very hard to find Dutch friends. . . . [S]he now avoids speaking German when out in the city, after noticing the reactions when her mother was visiting. Her Dutch is still poor. The experience reinforces her sense of not integrating, and encapsulates all the things that haven't turned out quite as she expected in the Netherlands. . . . She blames the integration failure on herself.[26]

Favell's conclusion after nearly ten years of interviews with European mobiles is simple: Living abroad in Europe, away from one's home, is a lonely life.[27]

That loneliness is a social cost of migration. But it points to economic costs as well. The social disconnectedness that often comes with migration can limit career and business potential. There can, of course, be niche advantages to bridging cultural divides. But people who have become successful at home are less likely to find advantage in moving across cultural gaps—either within the United States or across the world.

Social Capital as Information Exchange

One of the things social capital does is facilitate information exchange. For many at the top, information they glean from their social contacts can provide a valuable edge. Consider the distinction between "hard" and "soft" information.[28] Hard information is anything that can be put in a spreadsheet and e-mailed across the country. This kind of information tends to be quickly available to anyone in the market. Soft information has a more tacit character. Some things about a firm or a market can only be learned from walking the hallways and seeing how work teams operate or from being on the ground where the business transactions are happening.

Hard information is easily disseminated to a wide audience. Soft information travels more through interpersonal connections and social networks.

Insider status—having rich social networks in a place or field—brings timely and trustworthy soft information.[29] Outsiders are limited to the hard information that is largely accessible to everyone.

In some ways, the need for soft information has changed over time. Retail consumer lending, for example, used to be an industry that involved a lot of soft information, including personal interviewers and evaluations by loan officers. In some countries, this is still how consumer loans are decided.[30] But in the United States today, retail lending is now completely driven by hard information, with lending decisions made by computer algorithms.

Still, for many parts of the economy—especially at the elite levels— access to soft information remains a critical asset. In Silicon Valley, venture capitalists often follow an informal rule of investing in companies that are within a 20-minute drive of their headquarters.[31] This allows them to carefully monitor the companies in which they invest and to have multiple in-person meetings each week. Soft information remains critical to investment decisions. Access to soft information is a key reason why place-based social capital is important.

The role of social capital in the creation of elite income is often underappreciated. Income-earning capacity derives not just from individual talent, human capital, and work ethic, but also from social capital—social, professional, and business connections to colleagues, collaborators, and clients. Place is the foundation on which social connections form and replenish themselves over time—and it is how insiders are distinguished from outsiders. In this sense, place itself is a form of capital: Those who remain geographically close to their social networks can earn greater returns over time.

The Role of Technology

What about the promise of technology to allow one to work from anywhere? Some argue that new communication technology has meant "the death of distance."[32] Can elites use online communication to maintain their home-field advantage while moving around the globe?

Today, information moves faster between the United States and China than it once moved from one end of Manhattan to the other. With modern technology, instantaneous communication no longer requires physical co-presence. Internet connections now link up virtually every corner of the world to e-mail, file sharing, and video conferencing. Why don't elites just telecommute to work from a tropical tax haven?

This is an important question. If elites can produce income in a country while living abroad, then income may have effectively become mobile in the modern world. Why do the rich remain in a country despite the potential to work from anywhere?

Of course, some do telecommute to work, and knowledge workers are more likely to do so. Roughly one-third of American workers say they have "ever" worked remotely from home, allowing them to unbundle their geography of work and life for at least one day. On average, however, American workers telecommuted just 2.3 days per month in 2012. Moreover, telecommuting has hit a plateau, with no observable increase since 2006.[33] Telecommuting mostly serves as a way to bridge short, occasional absences from location. It is rarely an ongoing substitute for being co-present with other workers and colleagues.

In 2013, the Internet search company Yahoo! set off a public uproar of criticism when it banned telecommuting among its workers.[34] The reality, however, is that Silicon Valley companies are all focused on having their employees work alongside one another as much as possible. Companies like Google and Facebook use carrots rather than sticks: They invest heavily in creating workplaces where employees have no reason to leave. Google's main offices include games rooms, exercise facilities, ping-pong tables, pianos, mini-kitchens, washers and dryers for laundry, mobile services like haircuts, and 24/7 cafeterias with free food. Facebook has similar amenities with an open-floor design and no doors for offices, with the goal of fostering spontaneous, unplanned interactions. As one Facebook representative said, "You really can't walk through this space without bumping into people."[35] The irony is that Silicon Valley companies make the technology for telecommuting and distance communication, but they do not want their own people to use it—at least not for getting their work done.

Higher education is another area where new communication technology seemed poised to liberate people from place—until it did not. Sometime around 2010, the term "MOOC" was invented. It stands for Massive Open Online Course. MOOCs arrived with the promise of revolutionizing college education. MOOCs can scale up a classroom to any size, so a great professor can speak to any number of interested students who live anywhere in the world, at minimal additional cost beyond a conventional classroom lecture. Now, 1 million students can all take the best courses in engineering, computer science, economics, and sociology from the most gifted professors in the world. Top universities like Harvard, Princeton, and Stanford offer some of their best courses free to anyone with an Internet connection.

It has long been known that distance learning rarely works for students. The early hype around MOOCs failed to recognize this fact.[36] They arrived with the revolutionary ambition of overturning the entire system of college education. With a few years of actual experience, it became clear that online learning works only for a tiny fraction of students. Sebastian Thrun—the tech guru who pioneered the model—conceded that MOOCs are "a lousy product."[37] The course completion rate of MOOCs is around 5 percent, and most people who finish them already have advanced degrees. Young learners of the world are about as likely to spontaneously read Karl Marx's *Das Kapital* or Adam Smith's *Wealth of Nations* as they are to complete a MOOC.

The biggest challenge for students who want to become programmers, scientists, or writers is not the availability of information, but rather the motivation to devote hours to study—day after day, month after month, year after year. If we stacked up in one pile every book and article a student is expected to absorb in his college years, the mountain would seem insurmountable. College works best for students when it helps them sustain daily motivation for incremental learning.[38] And for most students, this works best when they are immersed in a social world where nearly everyone is focused on the same mission—a shared experience of pursuing knowledge, experimenting with topics, and building friendships that are layered around learning. Without a brick-and-mortar location that puts students in classrooms together, it is rare for students to complete even one course, much less four years of study.

The most elite universities of the world require their students to live on campus. More than 95 percent of undergraduates at Princeton, Harvard, Yale, and Stanford live on campus. At first glance, this seems anachronistic in the age of technology. It is hard to precisely articulate why physical co-presence—being part of a community focused on the same mission—is so much more effective than video chatting and file sharing among students spread around the world. But it speaks to the problem of telecommuting. Why don't elites just telecommute to work? By the same token, why don't the children of elites telecommute to their private school or Ivy League university from the same tropical tax haven where their parents ought to live?

People who are physically in a location have large benefits and advantages over those who check in remotely. Being a resident student in college is fundamentally different from telecommuting into class from Bermuda. People who Skype in are disconnected from the life of a place. Modern communication technology has become an integral part of our lives. But technology is complementary to—rather than a substitute for—face-to-face interaction.

Advantages of Place

Elite incomes are sustained not simply through individual brilliance and hard work, but also through collaborative relationships and social networks that depend in part on being in a shared place. The mobile millionaire thesis rests on highly individualistic conceptions of how people make money—and how people become and remain top income earners. It ignores that people with top incomes already tend to be living in the place where their human capital—their skills, training, and knowledge—is best fitted with the local economy and earns its highest returns. This fit between skills and place is important to how people became top earners in the first place. Most importantly, the mobility thesis ignores the role of social capital: People at the top are often deeply embedded insiders who continue to make money and earn economic rewards because of social networks that place them close to the action. This includes connections to clients, colleagues, cofounders, and the many information streams that cohere around the hundreds of "weak ties"[39] and happenstance social connections that successful people accumulate throughout their careers. Top income earners have a home-field advantage that would be diluted by moving away.

There are some celebrated cases of people like Mark Zuckerberg at Facebook who built tremendous fortunes at a young age. But most millionaires achieve their status and income through steady career advancement that puts them at the top of their game relatively late in life. These are the senior figures in business, finance, consulting, medicine, and law. For many top income earners, moving away could well lower their tax bill, or reduce their housing costs, or change many particular aspects of their lives. But the advantage of remaining in the place where they built their career is often too high to justify a move—not, at least, before retirement.

Place is a form of capital. Place is not a unique form of capital wholly different from the human and social capital that define it. But place is a container for the location-specific aspects—especially of social capital. People with the most economic success typically have the greatest home-field advantage.

We often think of mobility as the freedom to move. By this definition, top income earners can easily afford to move across the country—or even around the world. This ability to pay for moving trucks and have a savings account to gamble on a new start makes migration seem like a luxury that is mostly available to the rich. From this view, migration is analogous to travel—a classic luxury good. This analogy with jet-setting travel is a big part of why millionaire migration seems so plausible on the surface: Of course rich people can move—isn't that what money is for?

But, mobility is better understood by focusing on who would be materially better off if they lived somewhere else. Instead of asking who is free to move, we'd be better off asking who has a reason or need to move. From this perspective, mobility and migration are a burden of the poor. Movers tend to be those who have a poor economic fit with where they live—where they earn below-market wages for their work. Geographic mobility is the world of strivers, those who are searching for success and have yet to find it. Migration is more of a "necessity good"—something born of need rather than desire. It is important to disentangle the idea of *travel*—which often signifies wealth and status—from the idea of *migration*, which is often less glamorous—reflecting hardship or entry-level status.

Millionaire mobility is low because of where millionaires fall at the intersection of these two aspects of freedom: Elites have great freedom to move but little reason to do so. Among those at the top, migration means moving away from proven success and giving up their home-field advantage. Business and professional success is often built on place-specific social capital.

For people who already have a successful career, the best move is usually to stay in their home field.

In places with progressive taxation, the tax rate rises as one becomes more and more successful. Simple neoclassical economic thinking suggests that people should be tempted to leave such places once they achieve high income status. But this fails to appreciate the reality of elites: Success is both cause and consequence of social and economic embeddedness. As people ascend the income ladder (and rise in the tax brackets), they simultaneously deepen their local social contacts, prominence, reputation, information sources, knowledge, and embeddedness that strengthen—rather than loosen—their ties to place. Progressive taxes tend to fall on the most-embedded insiders who have the least motivation to move away.

Movement in a World Without Borders

A central question for the millionaire mobility thesis is whether migration—moving across borders—should be understood as a luxury good or as a necessity good. Do people value the freedom of mobility, or do they want to avoid the burdens and pains of dislocation? When people are free to move, under what circumstances do they seize the opportunity?

National borders are often seen as barriers that "keep insiders in and outsiders out."[40] We tend to think that countries of the world are held together by national borders. Without them, people would spill across borders like a flooding river, and nations would lose their identity and their ability to set distinctive national policies.

The sense that borders are holding back tremendous migration flow is partly why the mobile millionaire hypothesis seems compelling, because, increasingly, these borders do not appear to apply to the rich. Elites today face few real fences in the world that block their movement. Almost any country will open its doors to people bringing significant income and wealth. Millionaires live in a world whose borders are largely open to them, should they wish to move.[41]

And yet they do not—at least, not in meaningful numbers.

This points to an unexpected insight: Under certain general conditions, open borders do not matter for migration. What matters much more is the opportunity differential between places: the potential for individuals to have a much higher standard of living somewhere else. The opportunity differential between most rich countries is too small to spark migration between them. Their residents have place-specific social and human capital where they live. They have little reason to give up those advantages to move abroad. This is true both for elites and the general population. Legal borders are not holding back migration flow between rich countries. Within the West, legal borders are not especially important.

Two case studies of mobility among the general population of rich countries helps drive this point home: the Schengen zone of the European Union and the situation of Americans living abroad. These cases show that freedom of movement—the ability to cross borders—does not by itself spur migration.

Case 1: Free Movement in the Schengen Zone

In 1995, a rare natural experiment occurred in world geography. A massive cluster of countries erased their common borders. This was the Schengen zone, which today includes twenty-six nations with a combined population of over 400 million—the United States of Europe. It was a striking moment: The border between Germany and France became a road sign, just like the border between New York and New Jersey or Wisconsin and Illinois. Citizens of the European Union "can now build lives—careers, networks, relationships, families—beyond the nation-state containers that once defined personal identity and personal history. . . . European freedom [gives] the right to move, travel, live, work, study, and retire without frontiers."[42]

Yet, the remarkable dissolution of internal European borders led to virtually no new migration among western European nations. The European Union offers a vision of what globalization looks like for people who already live in a rich country. As it turned out, few German citizens wanted to live in Spain, Sweden, the Netherlands, Portugal, Greece, or France—or vice versa. The legal borders of western European countries were not holding back any migration flow. Opening the borders and establishing EU citizenship rights were symbolically powerful. Indeed, today most Europeans cite free movement as the greatest benefit of European citizenship. But the new Schengen zone did not lead more people to live in different countries that were now open to them.

Today, citizens of the EU15, the traditional western European countries, almost universally live in their country of birth.[43] Less than 2 percent of western European populations are EU citizens born in a different western European country. In a typical year, only 0.3 percent of the EU population moves across national borders. European migration rates are roughly one-tenth the migration rate between U.S. states.[44] This is largely unchanged from the early 1990s, before the opening of borders or the advent of EU citizenship.[45] Just like U.S. millionaires and the world's billionaires, citizens of rich European countries in general do not have much interest in moving in a borderless world.

Who does move in a borderless world? Today, western European countries are host to more people who were born abroad than ever before. Almost 10 percent of the population in western Europe is foreign-born, up from only 4 percent in 1995. The fabric of European society has changed and become more international, but this is not from migration within the original Schengen zone. Instead, the past two decades have seen a tremendous growth in immigrants from developing countries, particularly Turkey, Morocco, and Algeria.

This is very much in spite of official policy: While there is full freedom of movement and migration within Europe, external borders were meant to be fortress-like and to strictly limit migration from abroad. Figure 4.1 shows the growth of the foreign-born population in western European countries from 1995 to 2014. The figure also includes the subset of foreigners from other western European countries—such as Germans living in France, British nationals living in Belgium, or Swedish citizens living in Spain. Rights of free movement within the Schengen zone contributed almost nothing to the growth of foreign populations in western Europe.

Movers from eastern Europe are an interesting case. In the mid-2000s, the European Union expanded to embrace some 100 million people living in eight eastern European countries. Economically, the difference between eastern and western Europe was about the same as the difference between Mexico and the United States today. Poland's average income, for example, was only 27 percent that of neighboring Germany, even after adjusting for differences in cost of living.[46] Relative living standards were even lower in countries like Bulgaria and Romania. The opportunity differentials—the gap in real eco-

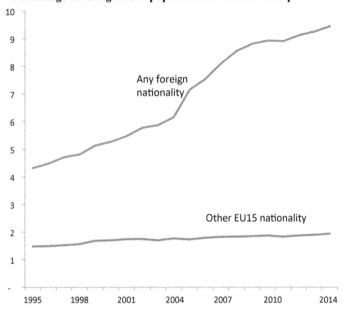

Figure 4.1. Foreign Population in Western Europe (EU15), 1995 to 2014. The figure shows the growth of the foreign-born population in western Europe; it also shows the subset of foreigners from other western European countries—such as Germans living in France and British nationals living in Belgium. Rights of free movement in the Schengen zone contributed almost nothing to the growth of foreign populations in western Europe. The visible bump in the foreign-born population after 2004 reflects the opening of the border to eastern Europe. However, less than 3 percent of eastern Europeans have exercised their right to live and work in the much richer countries of the West. Migration from outside Europe—primarily Africa—is what is really driving the growth of the foreign-born population in Europe. Source: Eurostat Data Explorer, "Population by Sex, Age, Citizenship, and Labor Status."

nomic life chances—between East and West were enormous. Observers rarely seem to acknowledge the unprecedented step Europe took in expanding citizenship rights to 100 million poor people. It was an experiment in world borders rivaled only by the original Schengen zone itself.

The visible bump in foreign-born population seen in Figure 4.1 after 2004 reflects the opening of the border to eastern Europe. Despite temporary restrictions on mobility, some 2.7 million eastern Europeans moved to western Europe as of 2014. Migration has been especially strong from specific countries. Poland has lost roughly 6 percent of its working-age population. Most striking is Romania, where 14 percent of Romania's working-age population—one in seven—now lives and works in a different EU country. But overall, fewer than 3 percent of eastern Europeans have exercised their right to live and work in the much richer countries of the West.[47] Despite the open borders, place remains sticky for the citizens of eastern Europe.

What really drives migration and the growth of the foreign-born population in Europe is immigration from Africa. This migration has nothing to do with the grand experiments in open borders and free mobility within Europe. It has been migration from outside Europe—from places where the border is officially closed but where opportunity differentials are extremely high. The foreign-born population of Europe comes from poor places where there is almost no chance of achieving Western living standards. These migrants have place-specific capital in their home countries that they leave behind when they move. But the opportunity differentials are such that being an outsider in Europe at the bottom of the economic ladder still offers better real pay than almost any possible job in Morocco or Algeria.

The experience of the EU and the Schengen zone tells us something very important about what borders do—and who moves in a borderless world. Between relatively developed countries, borders play a minimal role in migration patterns. If Europe and America dissolved their international borders and created a common EU–U.S. passport, allowing free movement within Euro-America, the outcome would likely be the same as for the Schengen zone: Americans would continue to live in America, and Europeans would continue to live in Europe.[48]

Legal borders are not what keep Americans in the United States or Europeans in Europe. Borders and immigration policies are not restricting the movement of people across places. Among rich countries, the limits to migration are overwhelmingly non-legal in nature. The central challenge is that other places are difficult and unwelcoming—migration often means giving up a lot of place-specific social capital. Without the push and pull of material need and greater economic opportunity, few people in well-off countries choose to live abroad.

Migration, in the end, is ultimately about opportunity differentials: the chance of living a better life in a higher-income country. Western Europe is a club of well-off countries. Any opportunity differentials between these nation-states are not large enough to outweigh the non-legal barriers to migration.

While there are differences in average wages across European countries, there are few tangible opportunity differentials. The good jobs in western Europe are typically not available to "foreigners," for reasons of language, culture, local knowledge, and social connections. Job access often requires place-based social capital. European migrants can often access only low-skill, low-wage jobs in other European countries. For most Europeans, moving would not offer an improvement in economic opportunities. Home-field advantage keeps people close to home.

The Brexit vote in Britain—the popular vote to exit the European Union—is a reflection of this. Few in England seemed to value their EU citizenship right to live and work anywhere in Europe, and losing this privilege was scarcely mentioned by the "Remain" supporters. It was a non-issue because virtually no Brits wanted to move to continental Europe. But many low-income eastern Europeans wanted to live in Britain, as did many poor immigrants who entered Europe from the developing world. There was, in short, one-sided interest in an open border.

Case 2: Americans Abroad

The experience of dissolving borders in Europe raises an interesting question for Americans: What would happen if U.S. citizens had free rights to live and work in other countries? Are the legal borders of other countries a tangible barrier to Americans, forcing them to stay in their home country?

No nation grants Americans the right to live and work in a different country without official permission. But, middle-class Americans—and certainly millionaires—could easily obtain residency and work permits in many nations if they so desired. This includes countries such as Norway, where real wages are much higher than in the United States—especially for lower- and middle-income workers. Alternatively, Americans might find an appealing niche economy and a high standard of living in many more tropical developing countries. Nevertheless, few Americans see an advantage to living abroad. Roughly 2.4 million Americans live in a different country, according to World Bank data.[49] In other words, less than 1 percent of Americans live outside their homeland.

The number of Americans abroad is an imperfect estimate. The U.S. Census does not enumerate citizens outside of the country, so estimates are derived from other countries' census reports. Such counts frequently exclude Americans who become naturalized citizens of other countries. And the counts can also include people we would not immediately think of as American expatriates. The growth of Americans in Mexico, for example, offers an interesting puzzle.

According to the 2010 Mexican census, 750,000 U.S.-born citizens live in Mexico. Moreover, the number of U.S.-born citizens in Mexico more than doubled over the past ten years.[50] Who are these American expatriates in Mexico, and what is driving their increase?

The North American Free Trade Agreement (NAFTA) expanded U.S. manufacturing into Mexico, so this may account for some Americans moving to Mexico. It is more tempting to think of the low cost of living in tropical places as drawing the mobile rich—or at least middle-class retirees—to Mexico. This brings to mind quaint colonial towns like San Miguel de Allende or beachside resorts with international airports like Puerto Vallarta, Cancun, and Los Cabos. The reality, however, is that most of the American expatriates are children.

The typical U.S.-born resident of Mexico is under 12 years old. These children are densely clustered in the impoverished border cities of Tijuana, Nuevo Laredo, and Cuidad Juárez.[51] Their parents are Mexican nationals. The growth of the U.S.-born population in Mexico is a story of large-scale return migration in recent years. Between 2009 and 2014, 1 million Mexicans moved back to their homeland—along with their U.S.-born children, who are U.S. citizens by birthright.

The number of American *gringos* living in Mexico is surprisingly small.[52] Only about 60,000 Americans have been issued permanent resident visas in Mexico, as of 2009.[53] Some additional number, no doubt, are "undocumented" in Mexico. And many more live part-time in the country, staying on tourist cards that are valid for up to six months.

American *travel* to Mexico is a large-scale industry. Americans made an estimated 20 million trips to the country in 2012, suggesting that about 6 percent of Americans travel to Mexico each year.[54] But remarkably few Americans make their home there. If we think about Americans born to American parents, this population approaches 300 million. Of those, only about 3 in 10,000 have made Mexico their primary residence.

Asymmetrical Borders

The world is a much bigger place than the United States. A large number of U.S. companies have expanded internationally, yet the number of U.S. citizens who have moved abroad is small. Still, it is hard to argue that national borders are what keep Americans at home.

The strict U.S. border with the rest of the world is in many ways asymmetrical and nonreciprocal. For example, the Tijuana–San Diego border crossing is notoriously congested, with lines that can last many hours. But pedestrians who travel from the United States into Tijuana do not face any screening, passport checks, or scrutiny of any kind. The pedestrian passageway from the United States to Tijuana is a completely open border. For American travelers, the biggest problem of entering Mexico is the burden of having to return through U.S. customs. The border between the two countries is asymmetrical, or a one-way valve: It aims to keep Mexicans out of the United States while allowing ready passage of Americans into Mexico.

The Tijuana border zone is emblematic of the asymmetrical borders of the modern world. Borders focus on limiting migration from South to North—stopping migration from poor countries to rich countries. There is less concern about flows in the opposite direction. Poor countries rarely use their legal borders to prevent American migration. And although poor countries do have some high-skill, high-income jobs, those positions are not filled by people from the West. America and the rest of the world are divided by an asymmetrically open border; Americans of reasonable means can easily cross it to live abroad more or less as they desire. Yet remarkably few choose to do so.

This is the case for American-born billionaires as well. As previously documented, only about 2 percent of U.S.-born billionaires live outside of the country. It is unlikely that foreign nations' legal borders—the barriers of obtaining a foreign visa—are keeping American elites in their homeland.

If this is what is meant by the new global mobility of the super-rich, the decline of the nation-state has been greatly exaggerated.

.   .   .

Many people are drawn to the idea of a jet-set life—being liberated from place, with the freedom to work and live elsewhere in the world. The image of "globals" evokes glamor, respect, achievement, and power.[55] The ideal of global mobility is not a Western value, nor one held more by the rich than by the middle class or the poor. Global mobility intrinsically speaks to basic notions of freedom, agency, and accomplishment.

Mobility, or at least the idea of being highly mobile and free from place-based constraints, confers status on those who appear to possess this option. However, the appeal of mobility—and the ease with which the rich can claim to be highly mobile—is based on a misunderstanding.

Within the rich OECD countries today, legal borders exist but do not seem to matter much. When the freedom to cross borders is established—either through elite income or Schengen zone policies—the residents of rich countries rarely move. Legal borders between places do not explain the homeland attachment of the rich—or even that of the middle class. Countries are held together by place-specific social and human capital. People in the West, rich or otherwise, rarely have much motivation to move. Places are a focal point for embeddedness and a container for social capital—a home-field advantage that is not very portable. Places are remarkably sticky—especially once people become successful in them—regardless of whether there is a legal border.

Millionaires and the Future of Taxation   5

What is the connection, in this time of globalization, between the rich and the places where they live? Are the rich today mobile millionaires—unplugged from place, state, and nation; ever ready to move; and no longer accountable to the policymakers of these traditional geographies? Or are the rich better understood as embedded elites—rooted in the places where they found their success and where they have become deeply connected insiders?

This question of millionaire mobility is central to the kinds of policies that places and nations can sustain in the twenty-first century. Rising inequality in the United States and most nations of the world means that taxable income is increasingly concentrated among the 1 percent of income earners. If this tax base is prone to flight, places will be under growing strain to retain and attract top income earners with lower taxes, undermining the revenue base for vital public services and infrastructure.

This book explores remarkable new big data on where the rich live and where they move. The IRS tax data from everyone in the United States who ever filed a million-dollar tax return between 1999 and 2011 includes 45 million tax returns from 3.7 million top-earning individuals. This gives unique evidence of how often the rich move across state lines and how many of these moves are to lower-tax states.

For an international view of the migration and attachment to place of the rich, I draw on the Forbes list of the world's billionaires. These data show where billionaires live, where they were born, how often they move after becoming wealthy, and how much national tax rates shape where they live.

The central finding of this book is that while millionaire migration and millionaire tax flight certainly occur, they are happening at the margins of social and economic significance. In the United States, millionaires move less than the general population: Their migration rates are lower than the middle class and much lower than the poor. The rich are more grounded in place than are lower income earners. Among the world's billionaires, the vast majority live in their country of birth, and only a small fraction—around 5 percent—move abroad after they amass their wealth. Millionaires and billionaires often have busy travel schedules, but few actually move their primary residence away from where they built their careers.

Among the modest set of millionaires who do move, income taxes matter, but less than one might expect. In the United States, almost all of the net millionaire migration to lower tax states is driven by movement into Florida. The Sunshine State systematically attracts rich people from high-tax states like New York, New Jersey, and Illinois. Other states with the same zero income tax system, like Texas and Tennessee, do not draw rich people from high-tax states. It is hard to tell how much taxes versus geography and climate make Florida attractive to the rich—although both probably matter.

Overall, the mobile millionaire thesis does not describe many rich people. As a group, top income earners are resistant to moving. This is partly because millionaires have family responsibilities that tie them to place: Compared to the general population, millionaires are much more likely to be married and more likely to have children at home. Millionaires are also much older than the typical person who moves across state lines.

Resistance to moving is also driven by a practical socioeconomic reality that income is partly tied to place. Unless one plans to retire, moving at the late-career stage often makes little financial sense. Moving means giving up a home-field advantage that helps sustain people's careers. Top income earners are mostly the working rich—such as managers, doctors, and lawyers. They can move their residence almost anywhere they wish, but it is more complicated to move their job and their income source to a lower tax state. Place is a form of capital for top income earners. Many of their competitive advantages are not portable.

Top-level income is often a joint product rather than a purely individual accomplishment. People with top incomes often have rich and layered connections to colleagues, collaborators, funders, and clients. These social, professional, and business ties lose much of their value when one moves away, and they are difficult to re-create in a place where one is relatively unknown. Migration often means walking away from place-specific social capital. The further afield one moves, the more one's social capital depreciates.

Top income earners also have specialized skills and knowledge—human capital—whose value is highest in certain places. New York is an ideal place to be an astute financial analyst, Boston is a great place to be a talented doctor, and Silicon Valley is the best place to be a brilliant programmer. Having one's skills in the right geographic place is key to achieving one's highest income potential. Florida and Nevada offer lower tax rates, but they also offer much lower returns to highly skilled labor. A central flaw in the mobile millionaire hypothesis is the assumption that top earners can make the same money anywhere they live. Human capital and especially social capital have place-specific returns, and moving to avoid taxes is unlikely to optimize what people can earn with their skills and abilities.

People who command the highest incomes rarely leave the places where they established their careers. Low migration among the rich is repeatedly documented in the tax returns of U.S. millionaires, in census data among the highly educated, and in the Forbes list of the world's billionaires. The rich largely live where they became successful. To be sure, most millionaires travel widely for business and leisure. They often retain teams of lawyers and accountants to probe the system for tax loopholes. But this does not render them a "transnational capitalist class" of global citizens beyond the reach of local or national policymakers.[1]

Neoclassical economic models misunderstand the reality of the rich and their connections to place. Conservative economists such as Martin Feldstein at Harvard have argued that states cannot pass progressive tax policies even temporarily without setting off large and painful outflows of top talent.[2] Many have used such simple economic models to predict that even modest taxes on the rich would result in millionaires moving by the thousands. The confidence of these predictions has been matched only by their inaccuracy—and by the lack of insight into how millionaires became top income earners to begin with. This boils down to a longstanding vice in neoclassical economic theory: assuming people to be frictionless agents willing and able to move their lives and their work around in a frictionless world whenever a new incentive arises.

Many of the same conceptual flaws have been embraced by left-leaning critics of globalization. The "transnational capitalist class" was presented by sociologists and political economists as the emergent elite of the twenty-first century. In this view, the rich have grown indifferent to nationhood: They traverse the globe with both impunity and guile and have become more powerful than the nation-states that haplessly attempt to govern them. The notion of a transnational capitalist class was never based on much more than anecdote and intuition, but it captured the imagination of many scholars on the left.[3]

The mobile millionaire thesis attracts interest and support from across the political spectrum. On the right, the idea of millionaire migration is appealing because it challenges the viability of high taxes on the rich, which conservatives oppose on general principle. On the left, millionaire migration feeds a narrative of greedy and unpatriotic elites pushing the tax burden onto the backs of the poor and the middle class. Both sides use anecdotes about millionaire migration to advance their ideological arguments. The left and the right draw on a shared narrative of the mobile rich that is largely untrue.

Improving Tax Policy

Based on the findings of this book, how should states set their tax policies? Should states raise taxes on millionaires? Could some states gain revenue by becoming tax havens for migrating millionaires?

The Revenue Gains from Millionaire Taxes

Imagine a tax policy in which millionaires pay an extra 1 percent of their total income in state taxes.[4] Further, suppose that only one state passes such a tax, and all other states keep their tax policies unchanged. What would be the long-term implications of this tax for millionaire migration in the United States? From the analysis using IRS tax-return data presented in Chapter 2, I can estimate the expected amount of migration for each percentage point of tax increase in a state.

Millionaire migration is low overall and only weakly affected by tax differences between states. So, the effects of such a tax would be small. For a typical state, passing this extra 1 percent tax would lead to roughly 12 fewer in-migrations and 11 additional out-migrations, for a long-run population loss of 23 millionaires. However, the typical state has a long-run population of more than 9,000 millionaires. Over a thirteen-year period, this millionaire tax would cause a drop of 0.2 percent of the state's millionaire population.

What does this mean for a state's fiscal balance? Critics often warn that taxes will cause more revenue loss from fleeing millionaires than they will bring in. A loss of 0.2 percent of the millionaire population means 99.8 percent of the millionaire population remains and is subject to the new 1 percent millionaire tax policy. The 23 missing millionaires would take with them about $2.4 million in tax revenue. But the remaining millionaires would contribute an extra $176 million in revenue. Despite the observed tax migration, the revenue gain from the tax is an order of magnitude larger than the revenue loss from migration.

By extension, a 10 percent millionaire tax would mean a loss of 2 percent of a state's millionaires. This is a greater loss, but the remaining 98 percent of millionaires would pay an extra 10 percent of their incomes in tax revenue. With such a tax, the typical state would raise around $1.8 billion per year, with a revenue loss from out-migration of only $24 million. One must always be cautious with such extrapolations, but it helps to clarify the relatively insignificant tax-migration effects. If the only argument against taxing millionaires is that they will leave, then states can proceed to raise top income taxes significantly without fear of revenue loss.

Does It Pay to Become a Tax Haven?

What if we think about this from the other direction—that of cutting taxes? Could some states pick up windfall gains by becoming tax havens for high income earners?

In general, cutting taxes on top earners generates massive revenue losses. Because so few millionaires are mobile, cutting taxes attracts only a handful of new millionaires. But, to attract those millionaires, a state has to cut the tax rate for a vastly larger population of embedded elites—the state's non-moving millionaires.

The only way states could use taxes to attract millionaires without devastating their budgets is through highly selective tax incentives. New Jersey tax officials, for example, could reach out to rich people who might want to move to New Jersey if the tax rate were lower. The state might offer a tax break to new millionaires who have never lived in New Jersey. New York would be a good place to look for such individuals, and surely some would take the deal. With such a policy, New Jersey could attract some new millionaires without having to cut taxes on its very large base population of resident millionaires.

The problem with this kind of selective tax break for movers is that other states will correctly see this as an opportunistic attempt to poach their tax base. If New York retaliates by offering a similar tax break to New Jersey millionaires, the state of New Jersey would probably soon regret having opened this door. The only real beneficiaries of this kind of tax competition would be the small group of mobile millionaires who get selective tax breaks for moving away.

In the United States, no state has attempted to lure millionaires away with selective tax breaks for people moving from out of state. But such a tax policy has been enacted on the international scene. Both Switzerland and Britain maintain tax loopholes for super-rich foreigners: They have progressive income taxes for their own citizens, but they allow rich expats to avoid the taxes of both their host country and their home country. These are essentially predatory policies that court elite migration by allowing foreigners to live by different and more favorable rules than those their domestic citizens have to follow. As noted in Chapter 3, a few dozen of the world's billionaires are taking advantage of these loopholes by residing in Switzerland and London, and probably thousands more of the lesser rich are doing so as well.

There is no principled defense of such policies even under the most "free market" economic thinking.[5] Countries can engage in legitimate tax competition by lowering their tax rates but not by offering special tax treatment to foreigners. Both Switzerland and Britain could reasonably face trade sanctions under World Trade Organization (WTO) rules of fair competition and equal treatment of locals and foreigners. Even modest sanctions—equal to the tax revenue losses these countries impose on other nations—would likely force the two countries to end tax breaks for rich foreigners, as the policies have limited benefits for citizens and voters in Britain and Swit-zerland.[6] This is a case where global trade rules, when enforced, could help maintain the integrity of national tax policies. Tax breaks designed purely to attract rich foreigners likely constitute an "illegal subsidy" under WTO trade rules.[7]

When states can only attempt to attract millionaires on an open playing field—by cutting rates on all top income earners—there is no credible busi-ness case for becoming a tax haven. If states wish to adopt Florida's income tax policies,[8] they must recognize that such a change will attract only a few millionaires and will sharply reduce the amount of revenue that many thou-sands of top earners are contributing to the state budget. The fiscal cost of becoming a tax haven is prohibitive. When this path is pursued, it necessar-ily means cutting infrastructure and services or raising taxes on the poor.

The fundamental problem facing states that want to attract the rich is that millionaire migration rates are very low. If the migration rate among mil-lionaires were ten times higher—say, 24 percent a year, rather than 2.4 per-cent—there might be a business case for cutting taxes on top incomes. But top income earners do not move very often, and taxes are not a big part of their migration decisions.

California and Kansas: Top Tax Rates and Fiscal Crises

The governor of Kansas, Sam Brownback, led a campaign to solve his state's budget problems by cutting taxes to stimulate growth and attract migration. Brownback insisted that "people move based on income tax rates," and his budget papers suggested that cutting income taxes would lead to higher rev-enue growth.[9] In 2011, Kansas passed a bill to lower its top tax rate from 6.45 to 4.5 percent; the bill also exempted many business owners from income tax entirely. Tax cuts to top earners were to be a "shot of adrenaline" to the state economy. It was pitched as a first step in a long-term goal of "getting to zero"—eliminating the income tax entirely, starting with tax breaks for the highest-income residents. The tax cuts set off deep revenue losses and an enormous budgetary hole. Escalating rounds of cuts to education and infra-structure followed.[10] In early 2017, the Kansas Supreme Court ruled that the state's education funding had fallen to unconstitutionally low levels.[11] The state's economy has remained flatlined, lagging behind most of the country in job growth. The "adrenaline" of top tax cuts did not achieve much more than devastating the state's budget.

In the same year Governor Brownback was elected in Kansas, Governor Jerry Brown was elected in California on a different agenda. Kansas and California have little in common, but they offer each other a glimpse of the path not taken.

Throughout the 2000s, California was becoming an ungovernable mess. Although constitutionally required to balance the state budget each year, California only did that twice in the decade. Hidden borrowing from other government agencies often made up the difference. With the national economic meltdown in 2008, the state's perilous fiscal position was revealed. The budget deficit ballooned to over $20 billion; the state was missing one-fifth of the revenue needed to operate. The state cut $15 billion in spending in 2009—some $8 billion of that from education. Day-to-day cash-flow problems emerged, and at one point the state actually stopped paying its bills—remarkably issuing IOUs instead. California's bond rating plummeted to the lowest level in the country.

As the budget crisis continued, some of the more troubling proposals included selling off the state parks to private interests and shortening the school year by twenty days. The University of California system raised tuition rates by 32 percent in a single year. Throughout the crisis, using taxes to address the problem was off the table: Tax increases required a two-thirds supermajority in the state congress, and the Republican minority would not allow it. *The Economist* magazine ran a special feature referring to California as a "failed state" and asking, "How can a place which has so much going for it . . . be so poorly governed?"[12]

After Governor Brown was elected in 2011, he asked voters to approve a tax increase on high incomes via the proposition system. The governor's Proposition 30, as it was called, would bypass the Republican blockade in the state congress. Voters approved the proposition in 2012, increasing the income tax on top earners substantially, including a 3-percent tax on the highest earners.

As of 2016, California has exceeded revenue projections for years, posting large year-after-year budget surpluses. The days of budgetary accounting games are over, the state fully paid off the deficit bonds issued by Governor Schwarzenegger during the crisis years, and it built up an $11 billion reserve fund. Independent budget scoring concluded that the state "is better prepared for an economic downturn than it has been at any point in decades."[13] Even Republican critics, despite reservations, acknowledge that the "soak-the-rich tax hike was a crucial budget healer."[14] Failed state no longer—California is back.

Collective Goods and Progressive Taxation

Any U.S. state can choose the path of higher and more progressive income taxes without causing an exodus of the rich. The "revenue-maximizing" tax rate on millionaires is higher than any state's current tax policy.[15] But many states do not want higher tax rates for the rich. States are collections of people deciding how much to tax themselves and how to share that tax burden. How much do people want collective public goods, such as infrastructure, schools, universities, safety nets, and transportation systems? And how much do people want private goods and individual spending power? In every state, people want some of both, and the political process is about getting the balance right. With this in mind, what is a reasonable way to share the cost of the collective goods we want?

Critics of progressive taxation have made a lot of fact-free arguments about the exceptional mobility of the rich. In the absence of tangible knowledge about millionaire mobility, people have continually made unrealistic claims to try to scare off serious policy discourse. In reality, the issue of tax migration is nearly irrelevant to the question of what state tax rates should be. Millionaire migration was a serious concern before we knew much about the migration behavior of top income earners. The mobile millionaire thesis turns out to have remarkably little empirical support—just enough to generate colorful anecdotes about millionaire tax flight, but not enough to be a real consideration in state tax policy.

There are two central questions for political discussion. First, what level of public goods versus private consumption do we want for our state? And second, what is a fair way to share the cost of our public goods? These questions provide a full docket for a sensible political dialogue. For example, there are reasonable debates to be had over whether states actually need more revenue. Countries like Sweden and France probably have little need for additional revenue, because of their already extensive provision of social services and public goods. In the United States, however, many aspects of education, public services, and infrastructure are in disrepair and lag behind other developed countries. U.S. policymakers need to focus on how best to address these problems through greater investments and improved efficiency.

Moral questions about tax fairness should also be more directly debated in the political sphere. Many people regard progressive income taxes as contrary to American values—as punitive measures against hard work and entrepreneurship that stem from a politics of envy. Many others believe that high income is a result of both effort and luck, and people with the greatest economic success bear greater moral responsibility to pay the operating costs of the American system. Open and honest debate around these issues is central to determining what level of progressive taxation is right for U.S. states.

Millionaire Taxes as an Intergenerational Transfer

Chapter 2 began with the story of New Jersey billionaire David Tepper moving to Florida. Tepper became emblematic in the press coverage of New Jersey's richest decamping for more favorable tax climates. Indeed, Mr. Tepper is not the only high-income resident who has moved to Florida. However, the coverage was excessive. Moreover, when millionaires move to states that charge them *higher* tax rates, such as when they move to California, it does not set off a media frenzy. A handful of prominent people, such as Oprah Winfrey, have moved from lower tax states to California in recent years. Yet, there were no media stories about how Oprah or others moved because they wanted to pay a *higher* state income tax. The only moves the media find interesting are cherry-picked examples of apparent tax migration. Full, comprehensive data on the migration of the rich gives a very different conclusion than the news media coverage.

It turns out that Mr. Tepper is not even a very good example of tax migration. Missed in all the media coverage is that Tepper is not actually from New Jersey. Tepper is a native of low-tax Pennsylvania, where he grew up and attended both college and graduate school. He moved to New Jersey—

where the top income tax rate is three times as high—to launch his investment business. He lived in the state for two decades, including twelve years after the New Jersey millionaire tax was passed, and he presumably paid a great deal of state income tax to New Jersey over the years.

Now heading into phased retirement, Mr. Tepper's move to Florida attracted much attention. Entirely missing from the coverage is that he moved from a state with a low, flat income tax to build a tremendous fortune in a high-tax state. New Jersey, despite its high-tax rate on the rich, produces a lot of millionaires; it is a good destination for young ambitious people to find success, and it has one of the highest millionaire concentrations (and one of the highest average incomes) in the country. The larger story of David Tepper is not so much about tax migration, but more about moving to a high-tax state to *achieve success*. If the press had reported Tepper's entire history of migration, this would have quickly tempered the impression that millionaires are leaving high-tax states.

Tepper moved to New Jersey many years before he knew how successful he would be and what tax rate he would be paying. This pattern of moving many years *before* achieving peak income is an important reality. Migration involves something of a Rawlsian "veil of ignorance" about the tax system. In the general population, people move across state lines when they are well educated but still young—usually some two decades before they hit their peak earnings phase. Among the world's billionaires, 16 percent live outside their country of birth, but two-thirds of this group moved at or before the beginning of their careers.

What kind of tax system would people want if they did not know whether they would be middle class or super-rich? Would the typical person care if there was a special tax rate on the super-rich? Most people who migrate are selecting where to live long before they know whether they will end up in the top tax bracket. Millionaires, in contrast, know what tax bracket they are in, but they are already rooted in place and have low migration rates as a result.

Because millionaires are usually late-career elites, a millionaire tax works as an intergenerational transfer. The tax draws revenues from the most successful members of the older generation as an endowment for younger people building their careers.

In a progressive income tax system, all people start life in the lowest tax bracket. Tax rates are low when people are beginning their careers and still have relatively low income. In America, highly educated young people are the most likely to move. They have high levels of education but do not yet have high income. They are not much concerned or affected by the tax rate on million-dollar incomes; if they ever make that much money, it will be decades in the future. People who ultimately become very successful will have to pay higher tax rates—but only once they achieve their highest economic aspirations. By the time people reach the height of their careers, their migration rates are dramatically lower than when they were young. The advanced-career rich are socially and economically embedded in the place where they live. Under a system of progressive income taxation, the highest tax rates fall on the least mobile individuals.

A recent interview study with the founders of the fastest-growing startup companies in the United States helps round out this point. The researchers, who interviewed 150 people from *Inc.* magazine's list of fastest-growing companies, sought to understand what the best entrepreneurs want in a city.[16] These founders had typically been mobile at some point in the past. But 80 percent of the founders had already lived in the area for at least two years before starting the company. For example, one founder was asked why he started his company in Park City, Utah. He replied, "My basement was located in Park City, and [the company] was started in my basement."[17] Park City is also a beautiful mountainous location, home to the U.S. Ski Team and the Sundance Film Festival.

The larger point is that the top startups in America were typically established wherever their founders happened to be living. Founders often spoke of urban amenities, the local talent pool, personal relationships, and access to their customer base as important to their company's location. But only 5 percent of founders mentioned the tax rate as a factor in where they chose to start their business. And once their business was established, 90 percent of founders kept their headquarters where they started out. In essence, once a startup is founded, it is already too late to try to lure it away with things like lower tax rates. If states want startup businesses, they need to grow them internally.

States have little ability to attract the highest income earners, but they can attract a pipeline of *future* top earners. One of the key components to a city's success, as management professor Richard Florida has emphasized, is its ability to cultivate, retain, and attract mobile young professionals.[18] To attract these young, highly educated, and motivated individuals, however, states should not focus on cutting the top tax rate. Top tax rates are not a salient issue for early career individuals, because these people are not in the top tax brackets. Instead, states should focus on creating quality of life and urban amenities that are attractive to the mobile young. This includes investing in affordable housing and education. Local universities create a pipeline of high-skill individuals, and good K–12 schools help retain them when they are ready to start a family.

In this sense, too, millionaire taxes are intergenerational transfers. Places can use higher taxes on the rich to fund services and amenities that are valuable to the young. In this way, the late-career rich can help endow a strong future for the next generation. And ensuring a city or state is a place where young college grads want to live can have reverberating positive effects on the older generation. In New York City, for example, many late-career and retired rich want to stay in the city to remain close to their children—who often want to be in the city for social and professional reasons.

Crucial to making a millionaire tax an effective intergenerational transfer is ensuring that tax dollars are spent well and used to fund more livable cities and states. This includes education and infrastructure that benefit the wider public, funding for science and advanced education that nurture innovation, and support for social programs such as mental health services that take the rougher edges off urban life. Evidence-based public policy—using big data to rigorously evaluate the effectiveness of policies and focus on the programs that most improve people's lives and opportunities—is central to maintaining support for progressive taxation.[19] If we can ensure good state governance that spends tax dollars wisely, everyone's children—rich and poor alike—can benefit from the higher-tax rates paid by the older generation of elites.

Intergenerational transfers are common in economic life and public policy. Medicare and Social Security—two of the biggest U.S. social programs—are intergenerational transfers that provide health insurance and income support to retirees paid for by taxes on the working-age population. Millionaire taxes are largely paid by late-career professionals. Using those revenues to support education and opportunities for the young parallels how professional families allocate resources within their own households. The upper middle classes and the rich deeply embrace the philosophy of "concerted cultivation" of their young—investing heavily in the development of their skills, confidence, and opportunities.[20] Millionaire taxes provide a way for states and cities to engage in the same kind of concerted cultivation of the young that we often see in professional families.

Millionaire taxes are often viewed through a lens of class conflict. Sociologist Monica Prasad has cautioned that political support for progressive taxation often fades when the emphasis is on class conflict.[21] The goal of redistribution can easily sound like retribution—a bitter, zero-sum politics that seeds its own backlash. This view of millionaire taxes is both counterproductive and empirically inaccurate. Combined with a commitment to evidence-based public policy, millionaire taxes are intergenerational transfers that support the ongoing vitality of places, states, and countries. Progressive taxes are paid by people with late-career success. The revenues pay for education, infrastructure, and public services that are most attractive to young, early-career individuals.

There is elegance to this system: Places provide infrastructure and services that are appealing to young professionals when they are most mobile, financed with a tax that the most successful of this class will eventually pay, but only in the future when they are an embedded, late-career elite. This intergenerational system of millionaire taxes is key to understanding why high-tax places—such as California and New York—can still thrive as centers for talent and elite economic success. These places train, retain, and attract talent when it is young, lower income, and mobile—and only make talent pay for the amenities as it becomes a successful elite with lives and careers enmeshed and embedded in place.

.   .   .

No one enjoys paying taxes. But in America, state budgets bear responsibility for kindergarten to grade 12 education, public universities, as well as much of the transportation infrastructure, social services, and police and judicial system. These systems make a big difference in our quality of life and in the opportunities available to young people.

We are living in an era of globalization, in which elites seem increasingly disconnected from the places where they live. But, this is largely a misunderstanding. Many industrial production systems have been offshored, although the professional and executive classes that manage these systems have not moved anywhere. Millionaires remain tied to where they live through career success and place-based human and social capital. They have a long accumulation of intangible capital that would be diminished by moving late in their careers to a place with lower taxes. The rich travel frequently for business and leisure, but rarely move away from the places where they found their success. Places and states are still central in holding elites to a social contract that upholds a commitment to shared prosperity.

The greater issue is that we are living in an era of rapidly rising inequality and diminished market opportunities for many. If we are to return to a time of shared prosperity—where the dividends of a productive society are enjoyed by many—millionaire taxes are part of the policy solution. It is still possible—indeed, about as much as ever—to tax the rich in this time of globalization. Combined with a credible commitment to use these revenues to support opportunities for the young, millionaire taxes can be part of a better future for all.

Notes

Chapter 1

1. Knight (2010).
2. Frank (2012).
3. Office of the Governor (2010).
4. See Sklair (2001).
5. See the classic works by Charles Tiebout (1956) and Richard Musgrave (1959).
6. Feldstein and Wrobel (1998).
7. Granovetter (1985), p. 487.
8. Saez (2016).
9. Mishel and Davis (2015).
10. Piketty (2014).
11. Noted international tax expert Reuven Avi-Yonah suggested this language back in 2001. See http://prospect.org/article/world-class-tax-evasion.
12. Martin (2013); for further analysis of elite influence on public policy, see Gilens (2012), Gilens and Page (2014), and Bartels, Page, and Seawright (2013).
13. These figures are from Piketty and Saez (2007), Table 2, p. 13. The figures are for 1970 to 2004 (the latest year they report on); if updated to 2016, there would be little real change. The figures represent average, rather than marginal, tax rates and include all taxes applied by the federal government, including the individual income tax, payroll tax, corporate tax, and the estate tax.
14. Andersen (2013).
15. Buffett (2010).
16. Cooper (2014).
17. Payne (n.d.), pp. 34 and 46.
18. Frank (2011).
19. Martin (2013).
20. Prasad (2012); Martin and Prasad (2014); Scheve and Stasavage (2016).
21. Sassen (2007), p. 65.
22. An initial look at these data is in Young, Varner, and Massey (2008). The

comprehensive analysis of millionaire migration in New Jersey is reported in Young and Varner (2011).

23. Young and Varner (2011).

24. The first report of research from this collaboration was published in Young et al. (2016). I drew on and extended these analyses in this book.

Chapter 2

1. Office of the Governor (2010).

2. Quoted in Erb (2013). Interestingly, in the 1960s the Soviet Union boasted of having entirely eliminated its income tax (Martin 2013).

3. Parker (2012).

4. Bartels, Page, and Seawright (2013), p. 53.

5. For more details on this data and the full technical analyses of it, see Young et al. (2016).

6. Later in this chapter, we'll look at people defined by exceptional wealth—the Forbes list of billionaires.

7. Property taxes are also important revenue sources for state and local governments. However, property taxes end up being fairly flat over the income distribution. The property tax may seem progressive on the surface. However, renters pay property tax as part of their rent, and low-income people pay more of their income on housing than do higher income earners. So, the key factors in the progressivity of state and local taxes in a state is the balance between the income tax and the sales tax.

8. U.S. Energy Information Administration (2013).

9. Ferrell and Reinke (2015).

10. Davis et al. (2009).

11. Ibid. In this text, "the poor" refers to the bottom 20 percent of income earners, and "the top" refers to the top 1 percent (making about $400,000). These estimates are for the year 2007.

12. Newman and O'Brien (2011), p. 122.

13. Davis et al. (2009).

14. Pearson (2014).

15. Quoted in Yamamura (2011).

16. Boltanski, Chiapello, and Elliott (2005), p. 155. Also quoted in Costas (2013), p. 1469.

17. Ferrie (2005); Molloy, Smith, and Wozniak (2011).

18. States rarely have the same tax rate to the exact decimal place. Here, I say that a state has a different (higher or lower) tax rate if the difference is 1 percentage point or more.

19. See Agrawal and Foremny (2016) for comparable research using big data on top income earners in Spain. They find very similar results.

20. Davis et al. (2015), p. 48.

21. Pearson (2014).

22. It is worth noting that business owners may find it easier to simultaneously move both their residence and their job to a different place.

23. Pearson (2014).

24. Technically, Wyoming and Montana have the highest number of Forbes billionaires per capita. Each state has 4 billionaires, which gives them a very large billionaire rate because of the extremely small base population in these states. In terms of tax policy, Wyoming has no state income tax, but Montana's income tax is at the U.S. average. These states have drawn largely retired billionaires attracted, in part, by the appeal of the Big Sky ranching country and Rocky Mountain ski resorts.

25. Five-year migration rates were reported in the 2005 Current Population Survey.

26. Greenstone and Looney (2012). For a deeper discussion of this, see "Family Structure and the Reproduction of Inequalities" by McLanahan and Percheski (2008).

27. My access to the IRS tax returns did not include data on occupation. These occupational breakdowns come from a separate study using IRS tax return data, by Bakija, Cole, and Heim (2009). These numbers are for 2005 (their most recent year) and refer to the top 0.1 percent of the income distribution (which is a bit higher than $1 million in income).

28. ESPN.com News Services (2013).

29. Daily Mail Reporter (2013).

30. Finley (2015).

31. Bakija, Cole, and Heim (2009), Table 5.

32. The very highest point of migration in Figure 2.7 is for youth ages 18 to 24 with a master's degree or higher. These folks are a pretty rare group. In practice, they are 23–24 years old with a master's degree. At Stanford, I've had the pleasure of teaching many such individuals—students who take a "co-terminal" master's degree as their fifth year of university.

33. Hirschman (1970).

34. Quoted in Young and Varner (2014), p. 4.

35. Carruthers and Lamoreaux (2016), p. 89.

Chapter 3

1. For one of the leading statements on the transnational capitalist class, see Sklair (2001); for recent more writings, see Carroll (2010) and Burris and Staples (2012).

2. Carroll (2010), p. 4.

3. Freeland (2012), p. 67.

4. Their billionaire status is defined by net worth, rather than by income. However, these individuals have high incomes as well. Even if they earn only 5 percent a year on their assets, that would imply incomes of $50 million per year for each $1 billion in wealth.

5. Paris (2013), p. 97.

6. Dolan (2012).

7. United Nations (2016).

8. Hunter, Oswald, and Charlton (2009).

9. Ioannidis (2004). International mobility is lower in medicine and the general social sciences (around 20 percent). Overall, 32 percent of highly cited scientists worldwide live outside their country of birth, according to Ioannidis (2004).

10. Ball (2015).

11. Meyer (2015).

12. For this calculation, I estimate the annual housing costs of a $16 million condo in Geneva to be roughly $750,000. Five times this amount is $4 million. For more details, see Broom and Hoffman (2014).

13. Allen (2014).

14. This number takes into account the 24 people for whom the timing of migration is unknown. I assume that a third of them moved after they became successful, equal to the share among the 142 billionaires for whom the timing of migration is known.

15. See Akcigit, Baslandze, and Stantcheva (2016) for a new study on the international mobility of top inventors (those with highly cited patents). They find essentially zero tax migration among "domestic" inventors who make up 95 percent of their global inventor population. Among inventors who have previously lived and worked abroad (who make up 5 percent of their sample), they find strong tax-migration effects. This fits well with my conclusion that there is a small subset of highly mobile elites who provide a steady stream of anecdotes about elite migration but are otherwise scarcely representative of top earners overall.

16. Packer's engagement with Carey was called off in late 2016. He has since applied for permanent residency in Israel (*Haaretz* 2016).

17. Three returned home, but 15 moved away, for a net increase of 12 mobiles.

18. Carroll (2010); see also Burris and Staples's (2012) article "In Search of a Transnational Capitalist Class."

19. Pfeifer (2009).

20. Government Accountability Office (2013).

21. Johannesen and Zucman (2014).

22. Cribb and Oved (2016).

23. Lipton and Creswell (2016).

24. Slemrod and Bakija (2008).

25. Levi (1988), p. 52.

26. Described in the tax code in Internal Revenue Service (2016b). Reuven Avi-Yonah, Law Professor at the University of Michigan and one of the top academic experts on international tax evasion, has written about this in a number of articles. The most accessible is "The Shame of Tax Havens" (2015).

27. Internal Revenue Service (2016a).

28. Winters (2011), p. 222.

29. Scheiber and Cohen (2015).

30. Caplin et al. (2015).

31. Incidentally, a significant portion of "foreign" investment in America is actually just Americans investing in America from secret offshore accounts. See Zucman (2013).

32. Lipton and Creswell (2016).

33. The Tax Justice Network has advocated for the term "secrecy jurisdiction."

34. Allen and Tonkin (2016).

35. For a dark case study of shell companies hiding money from likely litigation and an ugly divorce—and tax avoidance for good measure—see Confessore (2016) "How to Hide $400 Million" in the *New York Times*.

36. Zucman's purpose in estimating the usage of tax havens by country was to estimate the total amount of tax revenue that nations of the world are losing to the offshore economy. The amount of tax revenue lost to offshoring depends on the tax rate of each country.

37. Goldman (2004).

38. Putin has railed against Russia's infamous offshoring, and in 2015, he created an amnesty program to help bring the money back onshore. Ironically, Putin himself is tied to billions of dollars in offshore accounts in the Panama Papers.

39. Interestingly, Asia—which for the purpose of financial wealth means Japan, China, South Korea, and Hong Kong—matches the United States in a very low rate of offshoring. These Asian countries represent a thorough mix of high- and low-tax rates, as well as advanced democracies and autocratic regimes. More detailed study of offshoring wealth among Asian countries would offer a compelling regional test of what motivates offshoring.

Chapter 4

1. In a similar spirit, see "A Space for Place in Sociology" (Gieryn 2000).

2. Massey et al. (1998). For specific estimates of how much immigrants make in the United States compared to what they earn in their home country, see Clemens, Montenegro, and Pritchett (2009).

3. Milanovic (2011). It is worth noting that 5 percent of the Indian population is a much larger group than 5 percent of the U.S. population. Breaking this down in more detail, about 3 percent of the population of India earns more in real terms than the poorest 1 percent in the United States.

4. For an accessible discussion of this, see Milanovic (2011), pp. 109–129.

5. Ashenfelter (2012).

6. Clemens (2013).

7. See the discussions in Simula and Trannoy (2011) and the classic statement by Mirrlees (1982) on this point.

8. Quoted in Nagourney (2013).

9. For one, state income taxes are deductible on federal tax returns. The real difference in effective tax rates is more like 8 percentage points after federal deductibility. Federal deductibility of state taxes gives states an incentive to have highly progressive income taxes, as a significant portion of the cost to state taxpayers is reimbursed by the federal government.

10. Kleiner and Krueger (2010).

11. Hall and Soskice (2001).

12. For classic treatments of the concept of social capital, see Coleman (1988); Granovetter (1995); Portes (1998); Putnam (2000).

13. Dahl and Sorenson (2012); Sorenson and Audia (2000); Michelacci and Silva (2007).

14. Ruef, Aldrich, and Carter (2003). See also Kwon, Heflin, and Ruef (2013).

15. Olson and Olson (2000).

16. Dahl and Sorenson (2012).

17. Groysberg (2010).

18. Quoted in Groysberg (2010), p. 66.

19. Kirk (2009). This is an example of negative social capital.

20. Rivera (2015).

21. Goldberg et al. (2016).

22. Khan (2011).

23. Rivera (2015).

24. Klekowski von Koppenfels (2014), p. 94.

25. Ibid.

26. Favell (2008), p. 147.

27. Ibid., p. 230.

28. Petersen (2004).

29. Powell, Packalen, and Whittington (2012).

30. Guseva (2008).

31. Stross (2006).

32. Cairncross (2001).

33. Jones (2015).

34. Amabile and Kramer (2013).

35. Boorstin (2015).

36. A good analogy is the "Twitter revolution" in Egypt, which came with great expectations in 2011 and seemed to herald an era where new communication technology would empower and liberate oppressed people. The reality on the ground in Egypt has been much more sobering for the potential of Twitter to end injustice.

37. Chafkin (2013).

38. Chambliss and Takacs (2014).

39. See Granovetter (1973).

40. Popescu (2012), pp. 9–10.

41. See, for example, Freeland (2012).

42. Favell (2008), p. 3.

43. It is worth noting that after the Brexit vote in the United Kingdom, this may soon become the EU14. But, traditionally the EU15 is made up of the following countries that were EU members as of 1995: Austria, Belgium, Denmark, Finland, France, Germany, Greece, Ireland, Italy, Luxembourg, Netherlands, Portugal, Spain, Sweden, and the United Kingdom. These countries are generally referred to as western Europe.

44. OECD (2012).

45. Recchi et al. (2003); Koikkalanien (2011).

46. World Bank (2016). These figures are for Poland and Germany in 1991. Real income in Mexico was 26 percent of income in the United States in 1991 and was still only 30 percent of U.S. income in 2014. NAFTA seems to have done little to close the income gap between Mexico and the United States. In contrast, relative income in Poland had increased to 41 percent of German income by the time of EU enlargement in 2004 and to 51 percent of German income by 2014.

47. The share of eastern Europeans among the EU15 population rose from 0.9 percent in 1995 to 1.9 percent in 2014.

48. There is, however, a clear difference in EU–U.S. migration, with many more Europeans in America than vice versa. In 2005, the OECD estimated that about 450,000 people born in the United States were living in Europe, compared to 4.6 million people born in Europe who were living in the United States (OECD 2005). Much of this is presumably due to Americans' limited exposure to other European languages such as German, French, or Italian. Over 50 percent of Europeans are conversational in a foreign language, with English as the most common by a wide margin. Some 38 percent of EU citizens are conversational in English (European Commission 2012). In contrast, only a quarter of Americans are conversational in a foreign language, primarily Spanish (McComb 2001). For example, in Germany, 55 percent of the population is conversational in English, but only a negligible fraction of Americans (2.5 percent) can converse in German (European Commission 2012). Europeans' stronger foreign language skills make it easier for them to live in the United States.

49. World Bank (2015).

50. Instituto National Estadística y Geografía (2011).

51. Ibid. Roughly 80 percent of the foreign-born population of Mexico were born in the United States. The average age of *all* foreign born in Mexico is 12. For those born in a different foreign country than the United States (such as Spain), the average age is 37.

52. Ibid.

53. As of 2009. See Klekowski von Koppenfels (2014), pp. 30–31.

54. U.S. Department of Commerce (2013).

55. Elliott and Urry (2010).

Chapter 5

1. Sklair (2001).
2. Feldstein and Wrobel (1998).
3. Sklair (2001); Burris and Staples (2012). It should be noted that Carroll (2010), working in the same tradition as Sklair, has strongly refuted the notion of a transnational capitalist class based on evidence from networks of corporate board members—who overwhelmingly come from the country in which a corporation is headquartered.
4. This is an "effective" tax rate, rather than a marginal rate. Moreover, one must take into account federal deductibility of state income taxes. Raising the effective tax rate for millionaires is roughly what California's Proposition 30 tax accomplished, which was about a 3-point increase in the marginal rate on income over $1 million. States considering tax increases need to calculate the total increase in taxes payable after federal deductibility.
5. Slemrod (2010).
6. Zucman (2015) advocates this approach for dealing with countries that float bank transparency rules and facilitate shell companies and tax evasion.
7. For example, Washington State's preferential tax breaks for Boeing were ruled in violation of WTO rules in 2016 (Tribune News Services 2016).
8. Note that the question about migration to Florida—whether it is about avoiding taxes or seeking out tropical luxury—is not completely settled. But surely some of it is motivated by taxes. To take a conservative position, here I assume that all of the migration to Florida is for tax purposes. This gives the evidence for tax migration the benefit of the doubt.
9. Kaberline (2015); Kansas Office of the Governor (n.d.).
10. Associated Press (2016).
11. Smith and Bosman (2017).
12. Kluth (2011).
13. Taylor (2015).
14. Skelton (2015)
15. Young et al. (2016).
16. Endeavor Insight (2014).
17. Ibid., p. 7.
18. Florida (2014). See also the excellent work of Moretti (2012).
19. See, for example, Chetty et al. (2014).
20. Lareau (2003).
21. Prasad (2012).

References

Abler, Ronald. 1977. "The Telephone and the Evolution of the American Metropolitan System." In Ithiel de Sola Pool (Ed.), *The Social Impact of the Telephone* (pp. 318–341). Cambridge, MA: MIT Press.

Agrawal, David R., and Dirk Foremny. 2016. "Relocation of the Rich: Migration in Response to Top Tax Rate Changes from Spanish Reforms." SSRN Working Paper.

Akcigit, Ufuk, Salomé Baslandze, and Stefanie Stantcheva. 2016. "Taxation and the International Mobility of Inventors." *American Economic Review* 106 (10): 2930–2981.

Allen, Matthew. 2014. "Voters Retain Tax Perks for Rich Foreigners." *SwissInfo*. http://www.swissinfo.ch/directdemocracy/lump-sum-initiative_voters-retain-tax-perks-for-rich-foreigners/41135066 (retrieved August 20, 2016).

Allen, Vanessa, and Sam Tonkin. 2016. "Emma Watson 'Used Offshore Company Named in the Panama Papers to Buy £2.8m London Home'—but Issues Statement Saying She 'Receives No Tax Advantage' from It." *Daily Mail*. http://www.dailymail.co.uk/news/article-3583350/emma-watson-s-included-panama-papers-harry-potter-star-revealed-british-virgin-islands-offshore-firm.html (retrieved August 23, 2016).

Amabile, Teresa, and Steve Kramer. 2013, July 24. "Working from Home: A Work in Progress." *Harvard Business Review*. https://hbr.org/2013/07/working-from-home-a-work-in-pr (retrieved August 29, 2016).

Andersen, Erika. 2013, December 2. "23 Quotes from Warren Buffett on Life and Generosity." *Forbes*. https://www.forbes.com/sites/erikaandersen/2013/12/02/23-quotes-from-warren-buffett-on-life-and-generosity (retrieved March 8, 2017).

Angrist, Joshua, and Adriana Kugler. 2003. "Protective or Counter-Productive? Labour Market Institutions and the Effect of Immigration on EU Natives." *Economic Journal* 113 (June): F302–F331.

Ashenfelter, Orley. 2012. "Comparing Real Wages." *American Economic Review* 102 (2): 617–642.

Associated Press. 2016, April 19. "Kansas Loses Patience with Gov. Brownback's Tax Cuts." *CBS News*. http://www.cbsnews.com/news/kansas-loses-patience-governor -sam-brownback-tax-cuts/ (retrieved December 5, 2016).

Avi-Yonah, Reuven. 2001. "World-Class Tax Evasion." *The American Prospect*. http:// prospect.org/article/world-class-tax-evasion (retrieved December 5, 2016).

Avi-Yonah, Reuven. 2015. "The Shame of Tax Havens." *The American Prospect*. http://prospect.org/article/shame-tax-havens (retrieved August 20, 2016).

Bakija, Jon, Adam Cole, and Bradley T. Heim. 2009 (revised 2012). *Jobs and Income Growth of Top Earners and the Causes of Changing Income Inequality: Evidence from U.S. Tax Return Data*. Washington, DC: U.S. Department of the Treasury.

Ball, James. 2015. "Non-Dom Status: Living and Working in the UK, Without Paying All Your Tax in the UK." *The Guardian*. https://www.theguardian.com/money/2015/apr/07/non-dom-tax-status-living-working-paying-tax-uk (retrieved August 20, 2016).

Bartels, Larry, Benjamin Page, and Jason Seawright. 2013. "Democracy and the Policy Preferences of Wealthy Americans." *Perspectives on Politics* 11 (1): 51–73.

Benton, Meghan, and Milica Petrovic. 2013. *How Free Is Free Movement: Dynamics and Drivers of Mobility Within the European Union*. Brussels: Migration Policy Institute.

Boltanski, Luc, Eve Chiapello, and Gregory Elliott. 2005. *The New Spirit of Capitalism*. London: Verso.

Boorstin, Julia. 2015, May 22. "Inside Facebook's Futuristic New Headquarters." *CNBC*. http://www.cnbc.com/2015/05/22/inside-facebooks-futuristic-new-head quarters.html (retrieved August 29, 2016).

Broom, Giles, and Andy Hoffman. 2014. "Swiss Vote to Abolish Tax Break for Rich Threatens Status." *Bloomberg*. http://www.bloomberg.com/news/arti cles/2014– 11–20/swiss-vote-to-abolish-tax-break-for-rich-threatens-status (retrieved August 20, 2016).

Buffett, Warren. 2010, June 16. "My Philanthropic Pledge." *Fortune*. http://archive .fortune.com/2010/06/15/news/newsmakers/Warren_Buffett_Pledge_Letter.for tune/index.htm (retrieved March 8, 2017).

Burris, Val, and Clifford Staples. 2012. "In Search of a Transnational Capitalist Class: Alternative Methods for Comparing Director Interlocks Within and Between Nations and Regions." *International Journal of Comparative Sociology* 53 (4): 323–342.

Cairncross, Frances. 2001. *The Death of Distance: How the Communications Revolution Will Change Our Lives*. Cambridge, MA: Harvard Business School Press.

Caplin, Mortimer M., Sheldon S. Cohen, Lawrence B. Gibbs, Fred T. Goldberg Jr., Shirley D. Peterson, Margaret M. Richardson, and Charles O. Rossotti. 2015, November 9. "Letter to the Honorable Thad Cochran, the Honorable Barbara A. Mikulski, the Honorable Harold Rogers, and the Honorable Nita M. Lowey: IRS

Appropriations for Fiscal Year 2016." http://taxprof.typepad.com/files/former -irs-commissioners-letter-on-agency-budget.pdf (retrieved December 5, 2016).

Carroll, William. 2010. *The Making of a Transnational Capitalist Class: Corporate Power in the 21st Century*. New York: Zed Books.

Carruthers, Bruce G., and Naomi R. Lamoreaux. 2016. "Regulatory Races: The Effects of Jurisdictional Competition on Regulatory Standards." *Journal of Economic Literature* 54 (1): 52–97.

Chafkin, Max. 2013, November 14. "Udacity's Sebastian Thrun, Godfather of Free Online Education, Changes Course." *Fast Company*. http://www.fastcompany.com /3021473/udacity-sebastian-thrun-uphill-climb (retrieved August 29, 2016).

Chambliss, Daniel F., and Christopher G. Takacs. 2014. *How College Works*. Cambridge, MA: Harvard University Press.

Chetty, Raj, Nathaniel Hendren, Patrick Kline, and Emmanuel Saez. 2014. "Where Is the Land of Opportunity? The Geography of Intergenerational Mobility in the United States." *Quarterly Journal of Economics* 129 (4): 1553–1623.

Clemens, Michael A. 2013. "Why Do Programmers Earn More in Houston than Hyderabad? Evidence from Randomized Processing of US Visas." *American Economic Review: Papers & Proceedings* 103 (3): 198–202.

Clemens, Michael, Claudio Montenegro, and Lant Pritchett. 2009. "The Place Premium: Wage Differences for Identical Workers Across the U.S. Border." HKS Faculty Research Working Paper Series RWP09–004, John F. Kennedy School of Government, Harvard University.

Coleman, James S. 1988. "Social Capital in the Creation of Human Capital." *American Journal of Sociology* 94 (Supplement): S95–S120.

Confessore, Nicholas. 2016, November 30. "How to Hide $400 Million." *New York Times*. https://www.nytimes.com/2016/11/30/magazine/how-to-hide-400-mil lion.html (retrieved January 27, 2017).

Cooper, Marianne. 2014. *Cut Adrift: Families in Insecure Times*. University of California Press.

Costas, Jana. 2013. "Problematizing Mobility: A Metaphor of Stickiness, Non-Places, and the Kinetic Elite." *Organization Studies* 34 (10): 1467–1485.

Cribb, Robert, and Marco Chown Oved. 2016, April 4. "How Offshore Banking Is Costing Canada Billions of Dollars a Year." *The Star*. https://www.thestar.com/ news/world/2016/04/04/how-offshore-tax-havens-are-costing-canada-billions -of-dollars-a-year.html (retrieved August 23, 2016).

Dahl, Michael S., and Olav Sorenson. 2012. "Home Sweet Home: Entrepreneurs' Location Choices and the Performance of Their Ventures." *Management Science* 58 (6): 1059–1071.

Daily Mail Reporter. 2013, January 23. "Tiger Woods Admits He Left California Because of High Tax Rates After Rival Phil Mickelson Apologizes for Saying He May Quit West Coast." *Daily Mail Online*. http://www.dailymail.co.uk/news/

article-2266830/tiger-woods-admits-left-california-tax-rates.html?ito=feeds -newsxml (retrieved August 28, 2016).

Davis, Carl, et al. 2009. *Who Pays? A Distributional Analysis of the Tax Systems in All 50 States*, 3rd ed. Washington, DC: Institute on Taxation and Economic Policy.

Davis, Carl, et al. 2015. *Who Pays? A Distributional Analysis of the Tax Systems in All 50 States*, 5th ed. Washington, DC: Institute on Taxation and Economic Policy.

Dolan, Kerry. 2012. "Methodology: How We Crunch the Numbers." *Forbes*. http://www.forbes.com/sites/kerryadolan/2012/03/07/methodology-how-we-crunch -the-numbers/#110385c15113 (retrieved August 19, 2016).

Dube, Arindrajit, T. William Lester, and Michael Reich. 2010. "Minimum Wage Effects Across State Borders: Estimates Using Contiguous Counties." *Review of Economics and Statistics* 92 (4): 945–964.

Elliott, Anthony, and John Urry. 2010. *Mobile Lives*. London: Routledge.

Endeavor Insight. 2014, February. "What Do the Best Entrepreneurs Want in a City? Lessons from the Founders of America's Fastest-Growing Companies." http://www.ilga.gov/house/committees/98Documents/RevenueAndFinance/Supple mentalData/What%20Do%20the%20Best%20Entrepreneurs%20Want%20 in%20a%20City_%20-%20FINAL.pdf (retrieved March 10, 2017)

Erb, Kelly Phillips. 2013, January 4. "Depardieu Accepts Offer of Russian Citizenship to Escape Higher Taxes." *Forbes*. https://www.forbes.com/sites/kellyphil lipserb/2013/01/04/depardieu-accepts-offer-of-russian-citizenship-to-escape -higher-taxes/#5dd475a04344 (retrieved March 10, 2017).

ESPN.com News Services. 2013, January 22. "Mickelson Regrets Comments on Income Tax." *ESPN.com*. http://www.espn.com/golf/story/_/id/8868333/phil-mick elson-says-regrets-airing-opinion-taxes (retrieved August 28, 2016).

Eurofound. 2014. *Labour Mobility in the EU: Recent Policies*. Luxembourg: Publications Office of the European Union.

European Commission. 2012. *Special Eurobarometer 386: Europeans and Their Languages*. Brussels: European Commission.

European Commission. 2014. *Erasmus: Facts, Figures & Trends*. Brussels: European Commission.

Eurostat. 2011. *Migrants in Europe: A Statistical Portrait of the First and Second Generation*. Luxembourg: Publications Office of the European Union.

Favell, Adrian. 2008. *Eurostars and Eurocities: Free Movement and Mobility in an Integrating Europe*. Malden, MA: Blackwell.

Feldstein, Martin, and Marian Wrobel. 1998. "Can State Taxes Redistribute Income?" *Journal of Public Economics* 68 (3): 369–396.

Ferrell, Christopher, and David Reinke. 2015. *Household Income and Vehicle Fuel Economy in California*. San Jose, CA: Mineta Transportation Institute.

Ferrie, Joseph. 2005. "The End of American Exceptionalism? Mobility in the U.S. Since 1850." *Journal of Economic Perspectives* 19 (3): 199–215.

Finley, Allysia. 2015, January 27. "How Tennis Stars Handle the Tax Man's Topspin." *Wall Street Journal*. http://www.wsj.com/articles/allysia-finley-how-tennis-stars -handle-the-tax-mans-topspin-1422401926 (retrieved August 28, 2016).

Florida, Richard. 2014. *The Rise of the Creative Class—Revisited: Revised and Expanded*. New York: Basic Books.

Frank, Robert. 2011, October 27. "Millionaires Support Warren Buffett's Tax on the Rich." *Wall Street Journal*. http://blogs.wsj.com/wealth/2011/10/27/most-million aires-support-warren-buffetts-tax-on-the-rich/ (retrieved December 5, 2016).

Frank, Robert. 2012, July 9. "In Maryland, Higher Taxes Chase Out Rich: Study." *CNBC*. http://www.cnbc.com/id/48120446 (retrieved December 5, 2016).

Freeland, Chrystia. 2012. *Plutocrats: The Rise of the New Global Super-Rich and the Fall of Everyone Else*. New York: Penguin.

Gieryn, Thomas F. 2000. "A Space for Place in Sociology." *Annual Review of Sociology* 26: 463–496.

Gilens, Martin. 2012. *Affluence and Influence: Economic Inequality and Political Power in America*. Princeton, NJ: Princeton University Press and the Russell Sage Foundation.

Gilens, Martin, and Benjamin Page. 2014. "Testing Theories of American Politics: Elites, Interest Groups, and Average Citizens." *Perspectives on Politics* 12 (3): 564–581.

Goldberg, Amir, Sameer B. Srivastava, V. Govind Manian, Will Monroe, and Christopher Potts. 2016. "Fitting In or Standing Out? The Tradeoffs of Structural and Cultural Embeddedness." *American Sociological Review* 81 (6): 1190–1222.

Goldman, Marshall I. 2004. "Putin and the Oligarchs." *Foreign Affairs* (November/ December issue).

Gonzalez-Barrera, Ana. 2015, November 19. "More Mexicans Leaving Than Coming to the U.S." *Pew Research Center*. http://www.pewhispanic.org/2015/11/19/ more-mexicans-leaving-than-coming-to-the-u-s/ (retrieved December 5, 2016).

Government Accountability Office. 2013, April 26. "Offshore Tax Evasion: IRS Has Collected Billions of Dollars, but May Be Missing Continued Evasion." *Government Accountability Office*. http://www.gao.gov/products/GAO-13-318 (retrieved August 20, 2016).

Granovetter, Mark. 1973. "The Strength of Weak Ties." *American Journal of Sociology* 78 (6): 1360–1380.

Granovetter, Mark. 1985. "Economic Action and Social Structure: The Problem of Embeddedness." *American Journal of Sociology* 91 (November): 481–510.

Granovetter, Mark. 1995. *Getting a Job: A Study of Contacts and Careers*, 2nd ed. Chicago: University of Chicago Press.

Greenstone, Michael, and Adam Looney. 2012. "The Marriage Gap: The Impact of Economic and Technological Change on Marriage Rates." *The Brookings Institution*. https://www.brookings.edu/blog/jobs/2012/02/03/the-marriage-gap-the

-impact-of-economic-and-technological-change-on-marriage-rates/ (retrieved August 28, 2016).

Groysberg, Boris. 2010. *Chasing Stars: The Myth of Talent and the Portability of Performance*. Princeton, NJ: Princeton University Press.

Guseva, Alya. 2008. *Into the Red: The Birth of the Credit Card Market in Postcommunist Russia*. Stanford, CA: Stanford University Press.

Guttentag, Joseph, and Reuven Avi-Yonah. 2005. "Closing the International Tax Gap." In Max Sawaicky (Ed.), *Bridging the Tax Gap* (pp. 99–110. Washington, DC: Economic Policy Institute.

Haaretz. 2016, November 29. "Police Looking into Ties Between Australian Billionaire James Packer and Netanyahu's Family." *Haaretz*. http://www.haaretz.com/israel-news/1.756072 (retrieved March 10, 2017).

Hall, Peter A., and David Soskice (Eds.). 2001. *Varieties of Capitalism: The Institutional Foundations of Comparative Advantage*. Oxford, UK: Oxford University Press.

Hirschman, Albert. 1970. *Exit, Voice, and Loyalty: Responses to Decline in Firms, Organizations, and States*. Cambridge, MA: Harvard University Press.

Hunter, Rosalind S., Andrew J. Oswald, and Bruce G. Charlton. 2009. "The Elite Brain Drain." *The Economic Journal* 119 (538): F231–F251.

Instituto National Estadística y Geografía. 2011. "Los Nacidos en Otro País Suman 961,121 Personas." *Informativo Oportuno: Conociendo . . . Nos Todos* 1 (2). Aguascalientes: Censo de Poblacion y Vivienda 2010.

Internal Revenue Service. 2016a. "Abusive Offshore Tax Avoidance Schemes—Talking Points." https://www.irs.gov/businesses/small-businesses-self-employed/abusive-offshore-tax-avoidance-schemes-talking-points (retrieved December 5, 2016).

Internal Revenue Service. 2016b. "Publication 519, U.S. Tax Guide for Aliens." *Internal Revenue Service*. https://www.irs.gov/uac/about-publication-519 (retrieved August 20, 2016).

Ioannidis, John. 2004. "Global Estimates of High-Level Brain Drain and Deficit." *FASEB Journal* 18 (9): 936–939.

Johannesen, Niels, and Gabriel Zucman. 2014. "The End of Bank Secrecy? An Evaluation of the G20 Tax Haven Crackdown." *American Economic Journal: Economic Policy* 6 (1): 65–91.

Jones, Jeffrey M. 2015, August 19. "In U.S., Telecommuting for Work Climbs to 37%." *Gallup.com*. http://www.gallup.com/poll/184649/telecommuting-work-climbs.aspx (retrieved August 29, 2016).

Kaberline, Brian. 2015, July 24. "Brownback Q&A: Jobs, Growth Have Been the Target, Not State Revenue." *Kansas City Business Journal*.

Kansas Office of the Governor. n.d. "The Brownback Pro-Growth Plan: Making the State Income Tax Flatter, Fairer and Simpler." http://lwvtsc.atwebpages.com/studies/kstaxes/Brownback%20Pro-Growth%20Tax%20Plan.pdf (retrieved December 5, 2016).

Khan, Shamus Rahman. 2011. *Privilege: The Making of an Adolescent Elite at St. Paul's School*. Princeton, NJ: Princeton University Press.

Kirk, David S. 2009. "A Natural Experiment on Residential Change and Recidivism: Lessons from Hurricane Katrina." *American Sociological Review* 74 (3): 484–505.

Kleiner, Morris. 2006. *Licensing Occupations: Ensuring Quality or Restricting Competition?* Kalamazoo, MI: W. E. Upjohn Institute for Employment Research.

Kleiner, Morris, and Alan Krueger. 2010. "The Prevalence and Effects of Occupational Licensing." *British Journal of Industrial Relations* 48: 676–687.

Klekowski von Koppenfels, Amanda. 2014. *Migrants or Expatriates? Americans in Europe*. New York: Palgrave Macmillan.

Kleven, Henrik, Camille Landais, and Emmanuel Saez. 2013. "Taxation and International Migration of Superstars: Evidence from the European Football Market." *American Economic Review* 103 (5): 1892–1924.

Kluth, Andreas. 2011, April 20. "A Special Report on Democracy in California: The People's Will." *The Economist*. http://www.economist.com/blogs/multimedia /2011/04/special_report_democracy_california (retrieved December 5, 2016).

Knight, Phil. 2010, January 17. "Nike Chairman: Anti-Business Climate Nurtures 66, 67." *The Oregonian*.

Koikkalanien, Saara. 2011. *Free Movement in Europe: Past and Present*. Brussels: Migration Policy Institute.

KPMG. 2016. "Individual Income Tax Rates Table." *KPMG.com*. https://home.kpmg. com/xx/en/home/services/tax/tax-tools-and-resources/tax-rates-online/indi vidual-income-tax-rates-table.html (retrieved Dec. 5, 2016).

Kwon, Seok-Woo, Colleen Heflin, and Martin Ruef. 2013. "Community Social Capital and Entrepreneurship." *American Sociological Review* 78 (6): 980–1008.

Lareau, Annette. 2003. *Unequal Childhoods*. Berkeley: University of California Press.

Levi, Margaret. 1988. *Of Rule and Revenue*. Berkeley: University of California Press.

Lipton, Eric, and Julie Creswell. 2016, June 5. "Panama Papers Show How Rich United States Clients Hid Millions Abroad." *New York Times*. http://www.nytimes .com/2016/06/06/us/panama-papers.html?_r=1 (retrieved August 20, 2016).

Martin, Isaac. 2013. *Rich People's Movements: The Grassroots Campaign to Untax the One Percent*. Oxford, UK: Oxford University Press.

Martin, Isaac, and Monica Prasad. 2014. "Taxes and Fiscal Sociology." *Annual Review of Sociology* 40: 331–345.

Massey, Douglas S., et al. 1998. *Worlds in Motion: Understanding International Migration at the End of the Millennium*. Oxford, UK: Clarendon Press.

McComb, Chris. 2001. "About One in Four Americans Can Hold a Conversation in a Second Language." *Gallup.com*. http://www.gallup.com/poll/1825/about-one -four-americans-can-hold-conversation-second-language.aspx (retrieved December 5, 2016).

McLanahan, Sara, and Christine Percheski. 2008. "Family Structure and the Reproduction of Inequalities." *Annual Review of Sociology* 34: 257–276.

Meyer, Beat. 2015. "An Expat's Guide to Swiss Taxes." *Expatica*. http://www.expatica.com/ch/finance/taxes-in-switzerland_101589.html (retrieved August 20, 2016).

Michelacci, Claudio, and Olmo Silva. 2007. "Why So Many Local Entrepreneurs?" *Review of Economics and Statistics* 89 (4): 615–633.

Milanovic, Branko. 2011. *The Haves and the Have Nots: A Brief and Idiosyncratic History of Global Inequality*. New York: Basic Books.

Mirrlees, J. A. 1982. "Migration and Optimal Income Taxes." *Journal of Public Economics* 18 (3): 319–341.

Mishel, Lawrence, and Alyssa Davis. 2015, June 21. "Top CEOs Make 300 Times More Than Typical Workers." Issue Brief 399. Washington, DC: Economic Policy Institute.

Molloy, Raven, Christopher L. Smith, and Abigail Wozniak. 2011. "Internal Migration in the United States." *Journal of Economic Perspectives* 25 (3): 173–196.

Moretti, Enrico. 2012. *The New Geography of Jobs*. New York: Houghton Mifflin Harcourt.

Musgrave, Richard. 1959. *Theory of Public Finance: A Study in Public Economy*. New York: McGraw-Hill.

Nagourney, Adam. 2013, February 6. "Two-Tax Rise Tests Wealthy in California." *New York Times*. http://www.nytimes.com/2013/02/07/us/millionaires-consider-leaving-california-over-taxes.html?smid=pl-share (retrieved August 28, 2016).

Newman, Katherine S., and Rourke L. O'Brien. 2011. *Taxing the Poor: Doing Damage to the Truly Disadvantaged*. Berkeley: University of California Press.

OECD. 2005. *Trends in International Migration 2004*. Paris: OECD Publishing.

OECD. 2012. "Mobility and Migration in Europe." In *OECD Economic Surveys: European Union 2012*. Paris: OECD Publishing.

Office of the Governor. 2010, March 16. "Remarks of Governor Chris Christie to the Joint Session of the New Jersey Senate and General Assembly Regarding the Fiscal Year 2011 Budget." http://www.state.nj.us/governor/news/addresses/2010s/approved/20100316.html (retrieved July 6, 2014).

Olson, Gary, and Judith Olson. 2000. "Distance Matters." *Human–Computer Interaction* 15 (2): 139–178.

Paris, Chris. 2013. "The Homes of the Super-Rich: Multiple Residences, Hyper-Mobility, and Decoupling of Prime Residential Housing in Global Cities." In Iain Hay (Ed.), *Geographies of the Super-Rich* (pp. 94–109). Cheltenham, UK: Edward Elgar.

Payne, Erica, and the Patriotic Millionaires. n.d. *Renegotiating Power and Money in America*. http://patrioticmillionaires.org/book/powerandmoney.pdf (retrieved December 5, 2016).

Parker, Kim. 2012, August 27. "Yes, the Rich Are Different." *Pew Research Center*.

http://www.pewsocialtrends.org/2012/08/27/yes-the-rich-are-different/ (retrieved August 27, 2016).

Pearson, Elizabeth. 2014. "Saying Yes to Taxes: The Politics of Tax Reform Campaigns in Three Northwestern States, 1965–1973." *American Journal of Sociology* 119 (5): 1279–1323.

Petersen, Mitchell A. 2004. "Information: Hard and Soft." *Kellogg School of Management.* http://www.kellogg.northwestern.edu/faculty/petersen/htm/papers/soft hard.pdf (retrieved August 29, 2016).

Pfeifer, Stuart. 2009, October 26. "Banking." *Los Angeles Times.* http://articles.latimes .com/2009/oct/26/business/fi-swiss26 (retrieved August 20, 2016).

Piketty, Thomas. 2014. *Capital in the Twenty-First Century.* Cambridge, MA: Belknap Press.

Piketty, Thomas, and Emmanuel Saez. 2007. "How Progressive Is the U.S. Federal Tax System? A Historical and International Perspective." *Journal of Economic Perspectives* 21 (1): 3–24.

Piketty, Thomas, Emmanuel Saez, and Stefanie Stantcheva. 2014. "Optimal Taxation of Top Labor Incomes: A Tale of Three Elasticities." *American Economic Journal: Economic Policy* 6 (1): 230–271.

Popescu, Gabriel. 2012. *Bordering and Ordering the Twenty-First Century: Understanding Borders.* New York: Rowman & Littlefield.

Portes, Alejandro. 1998. "Social Capital: Its Origins and Applications in Modern Sociology." *Annual Review of Sociology* 24: 1–24.

Powell, Walter W., Kelley Packalen, and Kjersten Whittington. 2012. "Organizational and Institutional Genesis: The Emergence of High-Tech Clusters in the Life Sciences." In John F. Padgett and Walter W. Powell (Eds.), *The Emergence of Organization and Markets* (pp. 434–465). Princeton, NJ: Princeton University Press.

Prasad, Monica. 2012. *The Land of Too Much: American Abundance and the Paradox of Poverty.* Cambridge, MA: Harvard University Press.

Putnam, Robert D. 2000. *Bowling Alone: The Collapse and Revival of American Community.* New York: Simon & Schuster.

Recchi, Ettore, et al. 2003. "Intra-EU Migration: A Socio-Demographic Overview." PIONEUR Working Paper No. 3.

Rivera, Lauren A. 2015. *Pedigree: How Elite Students Get Elite Jobs.* Princeton, NJ: Princeton University Press.

Rossman, Gabriel, Nicole Esparza, and Phillip Bonacich. 2010. "I'd Like to Thank the Academy, Team Spillovers, and Network Centrality." *American Sociological Review* 75 (1): 31–51.

Ruef, Martin, Howard E. Aldrich, and Nancy M. Carter. 2003. "The Structure of Founding Teams: Homophily, Strong Ties, and Isolation Among U.S. Entrepreneurs." *American Sociological Review* 68 (2): 195.

Saez, Emmanuel. 2016. "Striking It Richer: The Evolution of Top Incomes in the

United States (Updated with 2015 Preliminary Estimates)." Originally published in *Pathways Magazine*, Stanford Center for the Study of Poverty and Inequality, 2008 (Winter): 6–7.

Saez, Emmanuel, Joel Slemrod, and Seth Giertz. 2012. "The Elasticity of Taxable Income with Respect to Marginal Tax Rates: A Critical Review." *Journal of Economic Literature* 50 (1): 3–50.

Sassen, Saskia. 2007. *A Sociology of Globalization*. New York: Norton.

Scheiber, Noam, and Patricia Cohen. 2015, December 29. "For the Wealthiest, a Private Tax System That Saves Them Billions." *New York Times*. http://www.nytimes .com/2015/12/30/business/economy/for-the-wealthiest-private-tax-system-saves -them-billions.html (retrieved August 23, 2016).

Scheve, Kenneth, and David Stasavage. 2016. *Taxing the Rich: A History of Fiscal Fairness in the United States and Europe*. Princeton, NJ: Princeton University Press.

Simula, Laurent, and Alain Trannoy. 2011. "Shall We Keep the Highly Skilled at Home? The Optimal Income Tax Perspective." *Social Choice and Welfare* 39 (4): 751–782.

Skelton, George. 2015, November 26. "Despite California's Budget Surplus, Unions Eye Tax Hikes." *Los Angeles Times*.

Sklair, Leslie. 2001. *The Transnational Capitalist Class*. Malden, MA: Blackwell.

Slemrod, Joel. 2010. "Location, (Real) Location, and Tax (Location): An Essay on the Place of Mobility in Optimal Taxation." *National Tax Journal* 63 (4): 843–864.

Slemrod, Joel, and Jon Bakija. 2008. *Taxing Ourselves: A Citizen's Guide to the Debate over Taxes*. Cambridge, MA: MIT Press.

Smith, Mitch, and Julie Bosman. 2017, March 2. "Kansas Supreme Court Says State Education Spending Is Too Low." *New York Times*. https://nyti.ms/2lEAjVi (retrieved March 10, 2017).

Sorenson, Olav, and Pino G. Audia. 2000. "The Social Structure of Entrepreneurial Activity: Geographic Concentration of Footwear Production in the United States, 1940–1989." *American Journal of Sociology* 106 (2): 424–462.

Stross, Randall. 2006, October 22. "It's Not the People You Know. It's Where You Are." *New York Times*. http://www.nytimes.com/2006/10/22/business/yourmoney /22digi.html (retrieved August 29, 2016).

Tax Justice Network. 2016. "What Is a Secrecy Jurisdiction?" *Tax Justice Network*. http://www.financialsecrecyindex.com/faq/what-is-a-secrecy-jurisdiction (retrieved December 5, 2016).

Taylor, Mac. 2015, November 18. "California's Fiscal Outlook." California Legislative Analyst's Office.

Tiebout, Charles M. 1956. "A Pure Theory of Local Expenditures." *Journal of Political Economy* 64 (5): 416–424.

Tribune News Services. 2016, November 28. "Boeing Was Offered Billions in Illegal Tax Breaks, WTO Says." *Chicago Tribune*. http://www.chicagotribune.com/business/ct -wto-boeing-tax-breaks-20161128-story.html (retrieved December 5, 2016).

United Nations, Department of Economic and Social Affairs. 2016. "International Migrant Stock 2015." *UN News Center*. http://www.un.org/en/development/desa/population/migration/data/estimates2/estimates15.shtml (retrieved August 19, 2016).

U.S. Department of Commerce. 2013. *2012 United States Resident Travel Abroad*. Washington, DC: International Trade Administration, National Travel and Tourism Office. http://travel.trade.gov/outreachpages/download_data_table/2012_US_Travel_Abroad.pdf (retrieved August 19, 2016).

U.S. Energy Information Administration. 2013. "U.S. Household Expenditures for Gasoline Account for Nearly 4% of Pretax Income." *U.S. Energy Information Administration*. http://www.eia.gov/todayinenergy/detail.cfm?id=9831 (retrieved August 27, 2016).

Winters, Jeffrey A. 2011. *Oligarchy*. Cambridge, UK: Cambridge University Press.

World Bank. 2015, September 24. "*Migration and Remittances Data*." *The World Bank*. http://www.worldbank.org/en/topic/migrationremittancesdiasporaissues/brief/migration-remittances-data) (retrieved December 5, 2015).

World Bank. 2016. "GNI Per Capita, PPP (Current International $)." *The World Bank*. http://data.worldbank.org/indicator/NY.GNP.PCAP.PP.CD (retrieved December 5, 2016).

Yamamura, Kevin. 2011. "Plans to 'Tax the Rich' Hold Risks and Rewards for California." *McClatchyDC*. http://www.mcclatchydc.com/news/nation-world/national/economy/article24721153.html (retrieved August 27, 2016).

Young, Cristobal, and Charles Varner. 2011. "Millionaire Migration and State Taxation of Top Incomes: Evidence from a Natural Experiment." *National Tax Journal* 64 (2): 255–284.

Young, Cristobal, and Charles Varner. 2014. "Do Millionaires Migrate When Tax Rates Are Raised?" *Pathways* (Summer). http://inequality.stanford.edu/sites/default/files/media/_media/pdf/pathways/summer_2014/Pathways_Summer_2014_YoungVarner.pdf (retrieved March 10, 2017).

Young, Cristobal, Charles Varner, Ithai Z. Lurie, and Richard Prisinzano. 2016. "Millionaire Migration and Taxation of the Elite: Evidence from Administrative Data." *American Sociological Review* 81 (3): 421–446.

Young, Cristobal, Charles Varner, and Douglas Massey. 2008. *Trends in New Jersey Migration: Housing, Employment, and Taxation*. Princeton, NJ: Princeton University, Policy Research Institute for the Region.

Zucman, Gabriel. 2013. "The Missing Wealth of Nations: Are Europe and the U.S. Net Debtors or Net Creditors?" *Quarterly Journal of Economics* 128 (3): 1321–1364.

Zucman, Gabriel. 2015. *The Hidden Wealth of Nations: The Scourge of Tax Havens*. Chicago: University of Chicago Press.

Index

Note: page numbers followed by *f* refer to figures; those followed by n refer to notes, with note number.

academics, as segment of high-earner category, 37

African nations: migration to Schengen Zone from, 91; and offshore accounts as privacy tool, 63*f,* 64

Akcigit, Ufuk, 116n15

Algeria, migration to Schengen Zone from, 89

American Community Survey, 38

Apple Corp., 55

Arab oil wealth, and offshore accounts as privacy tool, 62–63, 63*f*

Ashenfelter, Orley, 70

Asian nations: rate of offshore account use, 63*f,* 117n39; wages vs. other countries, 70

athletes, professional, flight to low-tax states, 37

autocratic countries, and offshore accounts as privacy tool, 64

Avi-Yonah, Reuven, 116n26

Bacon, Louis, 54

Bahamas, tax rates, and billionaire migration, 48

Baslandze, Salomé, 116n15

Bermuda, tax rates, and billionaire migration, 48

billionaires: data sources on, 11, 32, 34, 44, 51, 97–98; importance of national ties to, 54; large amount of travel by, 32, 44; primary place of residence, 44–46, 54

billionaires, as embedded elites, 98; and difficulty of avoiding taxes, 65; nation-based social and cultural capital and, 54. *See also* place of residence, attachment to

billionaires, international migration by: from 2010 to 2015, 53–54; and billionaire concentration in wealthier Western countries, 50–51, 50*f;* as children or young adults before success, 51, 52, 107; claims about, 43; effect of tax rates on, 46–51, 47*f,* 53; largely anecdotal evidence of, 53, 54, 94–95; percentage moving after success, 52–53, 65; rate vs. death rate, 54; rate vs. other groups, 45–46, 46*f;* typologies of, 51–52; to U.S., 45 billionaires, U.S.: number per capita, by state, effect of income tax rate on, 33, 33*f*; states with highest number of, 32–33

billionaires, U.S., migration by: to Florida, 34; high level of freedom in, 32; to low-tax states, 33–34; to other countries, as minimal, 94

Birkenfeld, Bradley, 55–56

Blavatnik, Len, 52

borders: asymmetrical, 94–95; stemming south-north flow as primary function of, 94. *See also* state borders

borders, as main obstacle to international migration: asymmetrical borders and, 94–95; as common assumption, 87–88; and migration by wealthy, ease of, 43, 87; as mistaken assumption, 91; U.S. migration to Mexico and, 94. *See also* Schengen Zone

Branson, Richard, 52

Brexit, attachment to place and, 92

Brin, Sergey, 52

Brown, Jerry, 104–5

Brownback, Sam, 103

Buffet, Warren, 6, 7, 32

Bulgaria, economic opportunity differential with western Europe, 89

business: as geographically sticky profession, 46; limited portability of acumen in, 76

business ownership: as constraint on migration, 36, 36*f*; high rate of, among millionaires, 36. *See also* income, as anchored to place

California: balance of sales and income taxes in, 19; fiscal crises of 2000s, 104; impact of tax increases in, 104–5, 120n4; millionaires per

capita in, 20; number of billionaires in, 32; number of billionaires per capita, 33

California millionaire tax, increase in, 34, 120n4; impact on millionaire migration, 34; impact on revenue, 104–5; and income as anchored to place, 72; millionaire threats of flight from, 37, 41

Canada: rate of offshore account use vs. other regions, 63*f*, 64–65; wages vs. other countries, 70

Capital in the Twenty-First Century (Piketty), 5

capitalism, global variations in, 76

Carroll, William, 120n3

Carruthers, Bruce, 41

Cayman Islands, tax rates, and billionaire migration, 48

celebrities, and offshore accounts as privacy tool, 61–62

Census Bureau, U.S.: education data, 38; income data, 10

CEO salaries, increases vs. average workers, 4

Chasing Stars (Groysberg), 78

children: as factor inhibiting mobility, 3, 35–36, 36*f*, 41, 68, 98; high percentage of parenthood among millionaires, 35–36, 98

children, welfare of: as millionaire motive for addressing inequality, 7; and millionaire taxes as intergenerational transfer, 106–10

Christie, Chris, 2

cities, multistate, millionaire flight across borders in, 31–32

computer programmers, and location as key factor in income, 70–71

Connecticut: adoption of progressive tax, 20; number of billionaires per

capita, 33; number of millionaires
    per capita, 20
conservative commentators: on tax
    system, 66, 100; and transnational
    capitalist class, as concept, 100
Cooper, Marianne, 7
corporate offshore bookkeeping sys-
    tems, vs. individual offshore ac-
    counts, 55
corporate services complex, increasing
    concentration of, as constraint on
    millionaire mobility, 9
countries, cultural differences between,
    and cultural fit, 80–81
cultural fit: and attachment to place,
    79–81; effect on employment, 79–80

Dahl, Michael, 78
data sources: on billionaires, 11, 32,
    34, 44, 51, 97–98; on millionaires,
    10–11, 16–17, 97, 115n27
Denmark, tax rates, and billionaire mi-
    gration, 46–47, 47f
Depardieu, Gerard, 15
District of Columbia (DC), millionaires
    per capita in, 20

economic opportunities: decline of, and
    importance of taxing high earners,
    111; differential in, as primary mo-
    tive for migration, 69–71, 87–88,
    89–90, 91–92; in high-tax states, as
    pull for future high earners, 107–9,
    110
education: data sources on, 38; impor-
    tance of investment in, 103, 104,
    106, 109–10; and income, 37–38;
    limited portability of, 75; and mi-
    gration rates, 37–40, 39f, 108; and
    remote learning, as failed experi-
    ment, 83–85

Egypt, Twitter revolution in, 118n36
Ellison, Larry, 32
employment: cultural fit and, 79–80;
    and limited portability of human
    capital, 68, 73, 74–77; migration
    of future high earners in search of,
    107–9, 110. See also income, as an-
    chored to place
Europe: migration to U.S. from,
    119n48; open borders within, effect
    on migration, 69; rate of offshore
    account use vs. other regions, 63f,
    64–65; wages vs. other countries,
    70. See also Schengen Zone
Exit, Voice, and Loyalty (Hirschman),
    41

Facebook: as natural monopoly, 26;
    Saverin's move from U.S. to avoid
    taxes on, 35; and telecommut-
    ing, discouragement of, 83; and
    Zuckerberg fortune, 85
family responsibilities, as factor inhibit-
    ing mobility, 3, 35–36, 36f, 41, 68,
    98
Favell, Adrian, 81
Feldstein, Martin, 3, 8, 99
Florida: balance of sales and income
    taxes in, 19, 26; billionaire migra-
    tion to, 34; high tax rate for low-
    income individuals, 26; millionaires
    per capita in, 20; natural monopoly
    among states with zero income tax,
    26–27; number of billionaires in,
    32–33; number of billionaires per
    capita, 33
Florida, millionaire migration to, 107;
    factors other than tax rate, 25–27,
    98; high level of, 26, 98; by profes-
    sional athletes, 37
Florida, Richard, 109

Forbes' billionaire list: as data source, 11, 32, 34, 44, 51, 97–98; top of list in 2010, 32
Foreign Account Tax Compliance Act of 2010 (FATCA), 56
foreign investment in U.S., Americans investing from offshore accounts and, 117n31
France, high-profile examples of tax flight from, 15
Freeland, Chrystia, 43

gasoline tax, as regressive, 18
Gates, Bill: on Forbes' billionaire list, 32; frequent travel by, 44; and Giving Pledge, 6; primary residence in Seattle, 44
Gilens, Martin, 113n12
Giving Pledge, 6
globalization: increase in, as taxation challenge, 1, 65; limited effect on migration between rich nations, 68–69; millionaire mobility as assumed consequence of, 1, 2, 3, 53, 94–95
global tax on wealth: calls for, 5; practical complications of, 5, 8
Google Corp.: and avoidance of corporate taxes, 55; stock reporting requirements and, 60; and telecommuting, discouragement of, 83; wealth of cofounder of, 52
Great Recession: and California fiscal crises, 104; and crackdown on offshore tax havens, 56
Greece, tax rates, and billionaire migration, 47–48, 47f
Groysberg, Boris, 78
Gutseriev, Mikhail, 54

H-1B visas, 71

The Hidden Wealth of Nations (Zucman), 59
high finance, as geographically sticky profession, 46
Hirschman, Albert, 41
Hogan, Larry, 2
Hong Kong, tax rates, and billionaire migration, 47, 47f, 48
Howard, Alan, 53
human capital: definition of, 73; as increasingly place-specific over time, 75; limited portability of, and attachment to place, 3–4, 68, 73, 74–77, 85, 99, 111

IMF. *See* International Monetary Fund
income: as anchored to place, 36–37, 71–74, 85–87, 98, 99, 107, 108, 111; location of work as key factor in, 69–71
Income Defense Industry, 58–59
income taxes: progressive, debate on morality of, 8, 106, 110; as progressive, 17–18. *See also* state income taxes
India, income vs. U.S., 69, 70–71
inequality: millionaires interested in addressing, 6–7; postwar decline in, 4; taxation as solution to, 1
inequality, growth of, 1, 4; factors in, 4–5; and importance of taxing high earners, 97, 111; as not inherent in capitalism, 4–5
information exchange, social capital and, 81–82
International Monetary Fund (IMF), monitoring of international investments, 60
inventors, tax migration among, 116n15
IRS: ability to monitor most income, 57–58; budget cuts at, 59;

crackdown on offshore accounts, 56; income sources invisible to, 58–59; records on millionaires, author's access to, 10, 17, 97, 115n27; and UBS bank scandal, 56

Kamprad, Ingvar, 54
Kansas, effect of tax cuts in, 103–4
Khodorkovsky, Mikhail, 64
Khosla, Vinod, 52
Kline, David, 72
Knight, Phil, 2
Koch, Charles and David, 32
Kuwait, and offshore accounts as privacy tool, 62–63

Lamoreaux, Naomi, 41
Lasry, Marc, 52
Latin American nations, wages vs. other countries, 70
leftist commentators: on character of millionaires, 66; and transnational capitalist class, as concept, 100
legal education, limited portability of, 75
Levi, Margaret, 58
licensed occupations, limited portability of, 75
lifestyle. See quality of life
London. See United Kingdom
loneliness, as social cost of migration, 81

marriage: as factor inhibiting mobility, 3, 35–36, 36f, 41, 68, 98; high rate of, among millionaires, 35–36, 98
Maryland millionaire tax: governor Hogan on, 2; millionaire threats of flight from, 41
Massachusetts, millionaires per capita in, 20

Massive Open Online Courses (MOOCs), as failed experiment, 83–85
McDonald's, and location as key factor in income, 70
media, and exaggeration of millionaire tax flight, 106–7
media and arts, as segment of high-earner category, 37
medical training, limited portability of, 75
Mexico: border with U.S., as asymmetrical, 94–95; economic opportunity differential with U.S., 89, 119n46; U.S. migration to, as minimal, 93–94; U.S. travel to, 93–94
Mickelson, Phil, 37
Middle Eastern countries: and offshore accounts as privacy tool, 62–63, 63f; wages vs. other countries, 70
migration: costs and complications of, 28–29; decline with increasing age, 38–40, 39f, 75, 107, 108; economic opportunity differential as primary motive for, 69–71, 87–88, 89–90, 91–92; education and, 37–40, 39f, 108; higher rate among low-income individuals, 21–23, 22f, 38, 67, 68, 86, 98; between rich nations, limited impact of globalization on, 68–69
migration, international: accumulated social capital as obstacle to, 91–92; economic opportunity differential as primary motive for, 69–71, 87–88, 89–90, 91–92; U.S. outmigration, as minimal, 93–94. See also borders, as main obstacle to international migration
migration by billionaires, international: from 2010 to 2015, 53–54; and bil-

lionaire concentration in wealthier
Western countries, 50–51, 50f; as
children or young adults before
success, 51, 52, 107; claims about,
43; effect of tax rates on, 46–51,
47f, 53; largely anecdotal evidence
of, 53, 54, 94–95; percentage moving after success, 52–53, 65; rate
of, vs. death rate, 54; rates vs. other
groups, 45–46, 46f; typologies of,
51–52; to and from U.S., 45
migration by billionaires, within U.S.:
to Florida, 34; high level of freedom
in, 32; to low-tax states, rate of,
33–34
migration by millionaires: data on,
10–11, 16–17; factors other than
tax rate in, 25–27, 98, 107–9, 110;
high-profile examples of, 15; interstate, low rate vs. others, 21–23, 22f,
25, 38, 67, 98, 99, 103; little change
in rate of, 9; as migration between
rich countries, 68; other factors af-
fecting, 24–25; perceived ease of,
16, 87; before success, to high-tax
states with economic opportunities,
107–9, 110
migration by millionaires, effect of
state income tax rates on, 23–25,
98; as minimal, in model excluding Florida, 25–26, 98; predicted
migration per percentage point rate
increase, 100–101; and revenue effects of decreased taxes, 101–3; and
revenue effects of increased taxes,
100–101. See also millionaire tax
flight
migration by millionaires, to Florida,
107; factors other than tax rate in,
25–27, 98; high level of, 26, 98; professional athletes and, 37

millionaires: annual number of in U.S.,
17; average income of, 17; definition of for this study, 2, 10, 17;
desire of some to address inequality, 6–7; desire of some to resist
progressive taxation, 7–9; high concentration in mid-Atlantic region,
20; leftist view of, 66; majority of as
working rich, 32, 36, 59, 72–73, 98;
public opinion on character of, 16.
See also migration by millionaires;
other specific topics
millionaires, as embedded elites, 16, 98;
business ownership and, 36, 36f;
and decline of migration rate with
increasing age, 38–40, 39f, 75, 107,
108; demographic factors in, 34–37,
36f, 41; and difficulty of avoiding
taxes, 65; family responsibilities
and, 3, 35–36, 36f, 41, 68, 98; as
insufficiently understood, 99–100;
and millionaire taxes, effectiveness
of, 65, 111; and revenue effects of
decreased taxes, 101–3; and revenue
effects of increased taxes, 100–101;
tax incentives for migration and,
108; and threat of flight as largely
empty, 41–42, 99, 105. See also place
of residence, attachment to
millionaires, mobility of: as assumed
consequence of globalization, 1, 2,
3, 53, 94–95; basis in individualistic
conceptions of income, 85; confusion of frequent travel with, 9, 23,
86; increasing concentration of
corporate services complex and, 9;
largely anecdotal evidence of, 2, 3,
23, 53, 94–95, 105, 116n15. See also
migration by millionaires; millionaires, as embedded elites; Schengen
Zone; travel

millionaires' taxes, data on, 10–11, 16–17, 97, 115n27

millionaire taxes in U.S. states: as balance to regressive tax structures, 19; common perception of as punitive, 110; impact of increases on overall revenue, 100–101; impact of reductions on overall revenue, 101–3; as intergenerational transfer, 106–10; period of increase in, 34; predicted millionaire migration per percentage point increase, 100–101; revenue-maximizing rate for, 105; states with, 2, 6; as too politically controversial, 8; viability of, 8, 65; warnings about millionaire flight due to, 2

millionaire tax flight: across state borders, 26–32, 29f, 30f; across state borders in multistate cities, 31–32; evidence for, as largely anecdotal, 2, 3, 23, 53, 94–95, 105, 116n15; exaggeration of, 66, 106–7; high rates as trigger for, 3; as irrelevant in setting tax rates, 105; as largely empty threat, 41–42, 99, 105; marginal significance of, 98; pressure for lower tax rates to prevent, 1, 2–3, 99–100; and revenue reduction concerns, 1, 3, 8; state millionaire taxes and, 2. See also migration by millionaires, effect of state income tax rates on; offshore accounts

Monaco, tax rates, and billionaire migration, 48, 53

Montana, number of billionaires per capita, 115n24

MOOCs (Massive Open Online Courses), as failed experiment, 83–85

Morocco, migration to Schengen Zone from, 89

Mossack Fonseca law firm, 56–57, 61–62

NAFTA (North American Free Trade Agreement), and U.S. migration to Mexico, 93

neoclassical economists, on millionaire tax flight, 3, 99–100

Nevada: as competitor among states with zero income tax, 26; millionaires per capita in, 20

New Hampshire: as competitor among states with zero income tax, 26; tax rate vs. Vermont, 30

New Jersey: millionaire migration to Florida from, 26; millionaires per capita in, 20

New Jersey millionaire tax: author's research on, 9–10; governor Christie on, 2; high-profile examples of flight from, 15; and millionaire migration, 106–7

Newman, Kathy, 19

New York: millionaire migration to Florida from, 26; number of billionaires in, 32; number of billionaires per capita, 33; number of millionaires in, 107; number of millionaires per capita, 20

noblesse oblige, as millionaire motive for addressing inequality, 6, 7

Norquist, Grover, 8

North American Free Trade Agreement (NAFTA), and U.S. migration to Mexico, 93

North Carolina, tax rate vs. Tennessee, 30

O'Brien, Rourke, 19

OECD countries: crackdown on offshore accounts, 56; small rate of millionaire migration from, 9 offshore accounts: amount of assets held in, 60, 65; banking secrecy as primary point of, 60–61; as ethically and legally questionable, 65; nationality of owners of, 62–65, 63*f*; reasons for wanting banking secrecy, 61–65; techniques for estimating total amount held in, 59–60

offshore accounts for tax evasion: amount of assets held in, 65; vs. corporate offshore bookkeeping systems, 55; methods used by, 57–59; as one among several uses, 60–65; Panama Papers and, 11, 56–57, 62, 117n38; possibility of eliminating, as issue, 57; as type of millionaire flight, 11, 54–55; UBS scandal and, 55–56; U.S. and OECD crackdown on, 56; as useful only for very richest individuals, 59; use of shell companies in, 56–57

Olenicoff, Igor, 56

Oregon: millionaire tax, vote on, 2; Portland, and millionaire flight across urban state borders, 31; tax rate vs. Washington State, 30

Oregon border counties: millionaire density vs. Washington State border counties, 31; millionaire migration to Washington State border counties from, 28–29, 29*f*

Organisation for Economic Cooperation and Development. *See* OECD

Packer, James, 54

Panama Papers, 11, 56–57, 62, 117n38

Patriotic Millionaires, 7

physicists, rate of international migration vs. billionaires, 45–46, 46*f*

Piketty, Thomas, 5, 8

place of residence: as container for location-specific aspects, 68, 86, 95; as form of capital, 82, 86, 98; of millionaires, effect of state income taxes on, 20–21, 21*f*

place of residence, attachment to, 67; accumulated human capital and, 3–4, 68, 73, 74–77, 85, 99, 111; accumulated social capital and, 3–4, 8, 16, 34, 68, 73, 77–82, 85, 91, 95, 99, 111; billionaires' tendency to remain in country of birth, 44–46, 54; Brexit and, 92; cultural fit and, 79–81; home-field advantage and, 3–4, 68, 73, 76–77, 79, 85, 86–87, 92, 95, 98; and income as anchored to place, 36–37, 71–74, 85–87, 98, 99, 107, 108, 111; and success as team effort, 74, 77–78, 85, 99; technology as means of overcoming, 82–85. *See also* billionaires, as embedded elite; millionaires, as embedded elite; Schengen Zone; *entries under* migration

Plutocrats (Freeland), 43

Poland: economic opportunity differential with western Europe, 89; migration to western Europe from, 91

poor people: and economic inequality, limited focus on, 7; high rate of migration in, 21–23, 22*f*, 38, 67, 68, 86, 98. *See also* inequality

portfolio interest exemption, 58–59

Prasad, Monica, 110

privacy, as reason for using offshore accounts, 61–62

property taxes, flatness across revenue distribution, 114n7

prosperity, shared, U.S. prospects for, 4, 5, 111

public policy, evidence-based, as goal, 109

Putin, Vladimir, and Russians' use of offshore accounts, 63–64, 117n38

Qatar, and offshore accounts as privacy tool, 62–63

quality of life: as motive for migration by future high earners, 108–9; as motive for migration by wealthy, 26–27, 51, 54

Republican Party, commitment to lower taxes, 8, 104

resource curse, and offshore accounts, 64

Romania: economic opportunity differential with western Europe, 89; migration to western Europe from, 91

Russia: and offshore accounts as privacy tool, 63–64, 63f; wages vs. other countries, 70

salaries, increases for CEOs vs. average workers, 4

sales tax: balance of with income taxes, in state tax systems, 17–19; as regressive, 17–18; theoretical advantages of, 18

Sandell, Thomas, 52

Sassen, Saskia, 9

Saudi Arabia: and offshore accounts as privacy tool, 62–63; tax rates, and billionaire migration, 46, 47f

Saverin, Eduardo, 35, 40

Schengen Zone, 88–92; dropping of borders within, 88; and economic opportunity differential as primary motive for migration, 89–90, 91–92; immigration from Africa to, 91; large migration to, from developing countries, 89, 90f; migration from eastern to western Europe, 89–91, 90f; minimal migration within western European, 88–89, 91–92, 95

Schwarzenegger, Arnold, 105

Silicon Valley: awareness of social inequality in, 7; and income as anchored to place, 71–72, 99; investors' reliance on soft information, 82; and telecommuting, discouragement of, 83

Singapore, tax rates, and billionaire migration, 47, 47f, 48, 53

social capital: and access to soft information, 81–82; and attachment to place of residence, 3–4, 8, 16, 34, 68, 73, 77–82, 85, 91, 95, 99, 111; co-location with others and, 77–78; cultural fit as element of, 79–81; deepening of with time in one location, 87; definition of, 73; and economic opportunity, 77, 81–82; limited portability of, 68, 73, 77–79; as obstacle to international migration, 91–92; and success as team effort, 74, 77–78, 85, 99

soft information, access to, social capital and, 81–82

Sorenson, Olav, 78

Stantcheva, Stefanie, 116n15

state borders: differences in tax rates across, 30, 30f; millionaire flight across, 26–32, 29f, 30f

state income taxes: balancing with sales taxes, in state tax systems, 17–19; deductibility of, as incentive for progressive tax, 118n9, 120n4; effect on migration rates of general population, 25; effect on millionaires' states of residence, 20–21, 21f;

increase in, effect on overall revenue effects, 100–101; reduction of, impact on overall revenue, 101–3; stability over time, 20. *See also* millionaire taxes

state income taxes, effect on millionaire migration, 23–25, 98; as minimal, in model excluding Florida, 25–26, 98; predicted migration per percentage point rate increase, 100–101; and revenue effects of decreased taxes, 101–3; and revenue effects of increased taxes, 100–101. *See also* millionaire tax flight

states: average number of millionaires per 1000 residents, 20; cultural differences between, and cultural fit, 80; emotional attachment to, 29; with highest number of billionaires, 32–33; with highest per-capita number of billionaires, 33; high-tax, as places of high economic opportunity, 107–9, 110

state tax policy: balance of collective vs. private goods in, 105–6; and evidence-based, effective spending, 109; impact of tax cuts in Kansas, 103–4; impact of tax increases in California, 104–5, 120n4; and intergenerational transfers, arguments for, 109–10; irrelevance of millionaire tax flight to, 105; and millionaire taxes as intergenerational transfer, 106–10; and millionaire tax incentives, 102–3; moral issues in, 8, 106, 110; and need for increased revenue, 105, 110; and revenue effects of decreased taxes, 101–3; and revenue effects of increased taxes, 100–101; revenue-maximizing rate for millionaires, 105; value of quality of life improvements for future revenue, 108–9

state tax systems: balance of sales and income taxes in, 17–19; as universally regressive, 19

success, as team effort, and millionaire's attachment to place, 74, 77–78, 85, 99

Sweden, tax rates, and billionaire migration, 46–47, 47f

Switzerland: on nationality of offshore account owners, 62; tax incentives to attract millionaires, 102–3; tax rates, and billionaire migration, 48, 49–50, 53–54

taxation: as quasi-voluntary system, 58; as source of public goods, and residents' satisfaction, 3; of wealthy individuals, U.S. reduction of, 5–6. *See also* millionaire taxes; millionaire tax flight; state income taxes

tax havens, international. *See* offshore accounts

tax incentives for millionaires: dubious moral and legal status of, 102–3, 120n7; effect on revenue, 102, 103; and millionaires as embedded elites, 108; in Switzerland, 49–50, 53, 102–3; in United Kingdom, 48–50, 53, 102–3

Taxing the Poor (Newman and O'Brien), 19

tax loopholes: creation and exploitation of, 58–59; portfolio interest exemption as, 58

tax system: conservative portrayal of as overly-complex, 66; fair, debate on, 8

technology, as means of overcoming attachment to place, 82–85 technology companies, and corporate tax avoidance, 55

telecommuting: claimed potential for, 82–83; limited real-world interest in, 83

Tennessee: as competitor among states with zero income tax, 26, 98; millionaires per capita in, 20; tax rate vs. North Carolina, 30

Tepper, David, 15, 106–7

Texas: as competitor among states with zero income tax, 26, 98; number of billionaires in, 32–33; number of billionaires per capita, 33

Thiel, Peter, 52

threats of millionaire flight: by California celebrities, 37; as largely empty threat, 41–42, 99, 105; as means of exercising leverage, 41–42

Thrun, Sebastian, 84

transnational capitalist class: billionaires as, 43; development of, 2; largely anecdotal evidence of, 2, 3, 53, 54, 94–95, 99, 100, 105, 116n15, 120n3; leftists' adoption of concept, 100

travel: by billionaires, large amount of, 32, 44; confusion of millionaire migration with, 9, 23, 86; increasing ease of, and millionaire mobility, 2; by millionaires, large amount of, 15

Treasury Department, U.S., Office for Tax Analysis, IRS data provided by, 10, 17

trickle down economics, 5–6

Turkey, migration to Schengen Zone from, 89

UBS bank: number of American-owned accounts at, 56; tax evasion scandal, 55–56

United Arab Emirates (UAE): and offshore accounts as privacy tool, 62–63; tax rates, and billionaire migration, 46, 47f, 53

United Kingdom: and Brexit, attachment to place in, 92; tax incentives to attract millionaires, 102–3; tax rates, and billionaire migration, 47, 47f, 48–50, 53–54

United States: border with Mexico, as asymmetrical, 94–95; economic opportunity differential with Mexico, 89, 119n46; migration of billionaires to, 45; migration to Mexico, as minimal, 94; number of billionaires residing in, 45; number of citizens living abroad, 93; outmigration from, as minimal, 92–94, 119n48; prospects for shared prosperity in, 4, 5, 111; rate of offshore account use vs. other regions, 63f, 64–65; travel to Mexico from, 93–94; wages vs. other countries, 70–71

Vermont, tax rate vs. New Hampshire, 30

Walton, Christine, 32

Washington State: balance of sales and income taxes in, 19; as Bill Gates' primary residence, 44; as competitor among states with zero income tax, 26; number of billionaires per capita, 33; tax incentives for Boeing, 120n7; tax rate vs. Oregon, 30; Vancouver, and millionaire flight across state borders, 31

Washington State border counties: millionaire density vs. Oregon border counties, 31; millionaire migration to Oregon border counties, 28–29, 29f

Watson, Emma, 61–62
wealth, as more transportable than income, 72
Williams sisters (tennis professionals), 37
Winfrey, Oprah, 34, 106
Winters, Jeffrey, 58–59
Wisconsin, number of billionaires per capita, 33
Woods, Tiger, 37
World Trade Organization (WTO), and legality of tax incentives, 102–3, 120n7

Wyoming: as competitor among states with zero income tax, 26; number of billionaires per capita, 115n24

Yahoo!, banning of telecommuting by, 83

Zuckerberg, Mark, 40, 85
Zuckerman, Mort, 52
Zucman, Gabriel: on nationality of offshore account owners, 62, 63f; on purpose of offshore accounts, 60; on size of offshore tax haven industry, 59, 60, 117n36

STUDIES IN SOCIAL INEQUALITY

Editors
David Grusky, Stanford University
Paula England, New York University

SNAP Matters: How Food Stamps Affect Health and Well-Being
Edited by Judith Bartfeld, Craig Gundersen, Timothy M. Smeeding,
and James P. Ziliak
2016

Income Inequality: Economic Disparities and the Middle Class in Affluent Countries
Edited by Janet C. Gornick and Markus Jäntti
2013

Determined to Succeed? Performance versus Choice in Educational Attainment
Edited by Michelle Jackson
2013

Contested Welfare States: Welfare Attitudes in Europe and Beyond
Edited by Stefan Svallfors
2012

Improving Learning Environments: School Discipline and Student Achievement in Comparative Perspective
Edited by Richard Arum and Melissa Velez
2012

The New Gilded Age: The Critical Inequality Debates of Our Time
Edited by David B. Grusky and Tamar Kricheli-Katz
2012

Broke: How Debt Bankrupts the Middle Class
Edited by Katherine Porter
2012

Making the Transition: Education and Labor Market Entry in Central and Eastern Europe
Edited by Irena Kogan, Clemens Noelke, and Michael Gebel
2011

Class and Power in the New Deal: Corporate Moderates, Southern Democrats, and the Liberal-Labor Coalition
By G. William Domhoff and Michael J. Webber
2011

Social Class and Changing Families in an Unequal America
Edited by Marcia J. Carlson and Paula England
2011

Dividing the Domestic: Men, Women, and Household Work in Cross-National Perspective
Edited by Judith Treas and Sonja Drobni?
2010

Gendered Trajectories: Women, Work, and Social Change in Japan and Taiwan
By Wei-hsin Yu
2009

Creating Wealth and Poverty in Postsocialist China
Edited by Deborah S. Davis and Wang Feng
2008

Shifting Ethnic Boundaries and Inequality in Israel: Or, How the Polish Peddler Became a German Intellectual
By Aziza Khazzoom
2008

Boundaries and Categories: Rising Inequality in Post-Socialist Urban China
By Wang Feng
2008

Stratification in Higher Education: A Comparative Study
Edited by Yossi Shavit, Richard Arum, and Adam Gamoran
2007

The Political Sociology of the Welfare State: Institutions, Social Cleavages, and Orientations
Edited by Stefan Svallfors
2007

On Sociology, Second Edition
    Volume One: Critique and Program
    Volume Two: Illustration and Retrospect
By John H. Goldthorpe
2007

After the Fall of the Wall: Life Courses in the Transformation of East Germany
Edited by Martin Diewald, Anne Goedicke, and Karl Ulrich Mayer
2006

Lightning Source UK Ltd.
Milton Keynes UK
UKHW010344200619
344423UK00027B/291/P

9 781503 601147